WALKING TO THE SAINTS

Anne McPherson

NOVALIS

Paulist Press
New York / Mahwah, N.J.

Aurora Books
David Lovell

Business office:
Novalis
49 Front Street East, 2nd Floor
Toronto, Ontario, Canada
M5E 1B3

Phone: 1-800-387-7164 or (416) 363-3303
Fax: 1-800-204-4140 or (416) 363-9409
E-mail: novalis@interlog.com

Canadian Cataloguing in Publication Data
McPherson, Anne
    Walking to the saints: a little pilgrimage in France
Includes bibliographical references.
ISBN 2-89507-076-8

    1. Pilgrims and pilgrimages–France. 2. McPherson, Anne–Journeys–France.
3. Spiritual biography. I. Title.
BX2320.5.F8M34 2000   263'.04244   C00-900969-8

We acknowledge the financial support of the Government of Canada through
the Book Publishing Industry Development Program (BPIDP) for our publishing
activities.

Published in the United States, the United Kingdom and Ireland
by arrangement with Novalis by
Paulist Press
997 Macarthur Boulevard
Mahwah, New Jersey 07430

www.paulistpress.com

Paulist Press ISBN: 0-8091-4018-7

Published in Australia by Aurora Books
in association with David Lovell Publishing
300 Victoria St, Richmond 3121
Tel (03) 9427 7 311 Fax (03) 9428 4450

ISBN 1 86355 082 8

Cover and layout: Blaine Herrmann
Illustrations: Tony Urquhart
Editor: Kevin Burns

© 2000 Novalis, Saint Paul University, Ottawa, Canada

Printed and bound in Canada.

To RJM
fellow pilgrim

I learn by going where I have to go

Theodore Roethke, "The Waking"

— ACKNOWLEDGMENTS —

During the last five years, in which the writing of this book staggered along, halted, drew inspiration and began again, I have been particularly indebted to John Bentley Mays and to John S. Porter, who read drafts, commented lucidly, and steadily encouraged me to continue along the road.

Warmest thanks to Charis Wahl, who first read the manuscript and made important structural suggestions.

A great hurrah goes to Tony Urquhart, who tramped through sunshine and downpours with pen and paper to catch the essence of these great pilgrim sites.

To the editors at Novalis, Anne Louise Mahoney and Stephen Scharper, I owe thanks for their gracious, thoughtful handling of the book.

Finally, it has been a pleasure to work with Kevin Burns, who has been an erudite, careful and sympathetic editor.

— TABLE OF CONTENTS —

— PROLOGUE —

This is about a pilgrimage that has taken more than sixty years and isn't over yet. It is also another trenchant example of how things never turn out the way you intend.

From the time I was five years old I knew France to be an enchanted country, a place of dreams. The reason for that, I am quite certain, is the French bonnet. This is a child's fine golden straw bonnet, modelled after an adult style. It is lined in pink silk, and ties with broad pink satin ribbons joined by a rosette on the top. Tucked under the brim at the hairline is a cluster of tiny silk flowers. My great-aunt Ada bought it in Paris for my mother, who would have been the right age to wear it in about 1910. I can remember begging to be allowed to wear "the French bonnet" – it was always called that. There is a snapshot of me at the age of five or six wearing it, draped around a fountain in the city rose garden, scowling at the sun. My daughter wore it. It is in my guest room cupboard now, waiting to teach the next unborn generation about the special quality that clings to French things.

As I grew up, my French cultural horizon expanded beyond fashion. I struggled to play Debussy on the piano; his *La cathédrale engloutie* was my star turn, and I adored it. I read Mauriac with passion, then – in a clear change of direction – Camus, who became one of my enduring heroes in art as in life. Later on, Messiaen came second only to Bach as the composer most often played on the stereo. It was a proud day when I managed Messiaen's *Le corps glorieux* on the organ.

Long before this, at the beginning of the war, I acquired a French uncle. Aunt Doris, my father's much younger sister, went to teach English in Auxerre after graduating from university. She later went on to the Sorbonne for further studies. There she met Hubert Grigaut, who came back with her to Canada, where they were married. Hubert was a true-blue Parisian; his family, Doris implied, was quite a cut above ours, socially and intellectually. He was, however, warm, extraordinarily polite, and very happy. I remember once when Hubert and Doris were visiting he asked me to read something to him in French;

afterwards he complimented me on my accent. I hung on to that praise for years. Somewhere along the road since then I've lost ground. No one would mistake me for a French speaker these days.

Doris, Hubert and I used to talk about literature, music and art – rather, she talked and we listened. I found them fascinating, their world unknown, sophisticated beyond my ken. When they moved to Washington, where Hubert taught at Georgetown University, Doris immersed herself in their mutual passion, collecting eighteenth-century French drawings, pastels, porcelain and furniture.

After some thirty years together, Hubert died. A few years later, Doris, when she learned she had cancer, gave her finest pieces to the National Gallery in Washington and other museums with appropriate collections. In her will she left me, astonished, the rest of her ceramics collection – a bewildering treasury, now dearly loved. From the time of that first gift, about which I understood nothing whatsoever, to the present, when I've recently curated an exhibition of the ceramic work of a Parisian sculptor at the Gardiner Museum of Ceramic Art in Toronto, has been a voyage of discovery that would have pleased her, I'm sure.

By the time I graduated from university I had joined the ranks of young hopeful-intellectuals who went to French films – the *nouvelle vague* had just swept in, I tried to follow Julia Child's impossibly intricate recipes, and hung Monet posters on our walls. We planned our first trips to Europe, although mine wasn't to take place for another twelve years.

When it did occur, it fulfilled every imagining and then some. I remember that for our very first meal in France, taken in a small auberge somewhere near Rouen, we had trout that the owner had just caught up the river minutes before. This was in the days when the only fish you could buy fresh in Ontario was haddock, and the deep freeze offered flavourless sole or fish sticks. We bought a delicate chandelier, saw our first astonishing Roman ruins in Provence, found by chance in the dark one night a perfect inn on the shore of a Savoyard lake – still our favourite – and spent our last night in Paris listening to Bach's *B Minor Mass* in Notre-Dame. It was, as T.S. Eliot says, satisfactory.

Thirty-five years have passed since that first visit to France. During that time my husband Bob and I have travelled through most of the departments, except those in the northern mining district, filling our eyes and ears and stomachs with treasures aesthetic, religious, quaint, curious and *gourmandise*. We've rented houses in Provence, near Bordeaux, in the Basque country and in the Auvergne, and day-tripped in small circles outward from there. We've rarely had a bad meal or an undrinkable wine, or a bed we couldn't sleep in, or a town we'd rather not have seen. Nor have we heard more than a few snarly or abrupt words, nor even a break in the usual politesse. Our hosts have minded their own business, and have not been bothered that we were minding theirs too.

Somehow all of that must have penetrated the stiffer skin of these WASPy anglophones, enough to make us want more and more of it. Going to France became the reward, the nectar for the worker bees at the end of a year's efforts. So, as often as we could scrape together travel money, we came to France.

France was the perfect holiday place, set apart from real life, on the other side of the rainbow. It might have stayed that way, had we not decided fifteen years ago to buy a country house in Languedoc and begin to put down some roots. There were signs even before that, however, to indicate that living and travelling in France had more serious implications than just getting away from it all.

At home in Canada, while France was still being kept in a separate box as a holiday treat, I had begun to take my religious situation seriously. Having decided that religion was not something to be trifled with – either get it or get out – I immersed myself in it all, theology, meditation, ritual and music. Even for an Anglican such as I, however, there were certain anomalies and contradictions. The new theology, as it was called in the 1960s and 70s, raised some very important and disturbing questions about the hierarchical and triumphal structure of the Christian universe. Writers outside that universe, such as Camus, Sartre and Beckett, raised other questions, about meaning and morality. The feminist rethinking of theology was beginning to waft into my consciousness. There was the additional difficulty, or challenge as I saw it then, of being both an insider as a believer, and an outsider as student and teacher. At that time I was giving a university course in religion and literature, and doing post-graduate work in religious sciences. I loved the leap back and forth over the "objectivity" fence;

the view was tremendous and stimulating. The upshot was, however, that I was spiritually eager and at the same time theologically sceptical. A good place to be, if you like exercise.

The first hint that the France of my holidays could hold some spiritual significance for me came quite suddenly, and with it, that uncanny suspicion that what seems unplanned isn't really, it's just that the plan didn't come from my conscious mind. In the early 1970s the National Film Board of Canada produced a fine little film about the work of Jean Vanier, founder of the L'Arche communities for people whom he described as emotionally deprived, although their mental capacities were also diminished. The film was made in the environs of the first L'Arche – it means "the ark" – in Trosly-Breuil in northern France. Here, it seemed to me, were Christians behaving together as Jesus meant them to do, reaching out and embracing those without the capacity to reach out themselves. What was taking place at L'Arche seemed to me to be utterly beautiful.

Bob and I were planning to come to France by way of England that year, crossing the Channel to Boulogne, and then driving east and south. Knowing that we might be in the general region of Trosly-Breuil, I had looked for the village on our map, but with no luck. Oh well, we thought, if we had gone there, what would we have done or said? We'd have been intruders surely.

We spent the night in Compiègne, where Joan of Arc fought her last, unsuccessful battle and was taken prisoner. As we were driving south from there, I half glimpsed a sign out of the car window and shouted for Bob to stop. The sign said Trosly. Could it be? A little further along we saw a tapering *allée* of plane trees running along a field, looking just like the ones that had figured so prominently in the film. Then, a few hundred metres on, after entering a village whose sign said Breuil, we saw a long, lean figure of a man walking, his arm thrown over the shoulders of a shorter man. We stopped abruptly and, without giving myself time to think about it and get nervous, I ran across the road to say hello to M. Vanier.

He was kindness itself. I told him we had only the day, and would love to be able to make a visit if it wouldn't inconvenience anyone. Of course. He invited us to follow him up to the main house, where he made arrangements for us to go to the visitors' house for lunch, and found us a guide to take us around after lunch. We ate with a group of volunteers and residents. We sang songs, did the dishes; we were the only guests. We saw everything – the print shop, the shop where they made small ceramic religious pieces, the workshop where they assembled metal parts for an automotive factory. We visited one of the houses in which several residents live with one or two volunteers *en famille*. Everywhere in this village where Vanier has gradually bought houses to take in more and more residents, the feeling was one of simplicity, not poverty. This was living on a shoestring, certainly, but that was not what we saw. Instead it was the importance of a safe, creative, warm life in which shrieks of anger, moaning pain and unexpected bursts of laughter might emerge and be accepted.

Throwing our plans right out of whack, we stayed for evening mass, which was held in an old barn converted to a chapel, though bearing all the cracks, chinks and stains of an earlier life. The ancient priest, Vanier's original mentor, celebrated the mass from his chair. Jean Vanier sat on a cushion on the floor in the front row among his "boys." We sat in the bleachers next to a young man who kept going out periodically to ride his bike around the barnyard and then coming back to his seat. No one seemed bothered by this, nor by the outpourings of another member of this chosen family who spoke up vehemently from time to time. Hugs were given, hands were held, smiles were coaxed from solemn-eyed, hesitant people, although many seemed too shy or absorbed in some internal distance to respond. It was perhaps the most moving experience of a community of love and worship either of us had ever had. It put Jean Vanier into my small, personally elected circle of modern-day saints. It also made both of us wish that we had the French and the character – mainly the character – to sign on there for a time, knowing we'd gain far more than we'd give. I remember that after we drove away we didn't speak for a long time, trying to register and hold dear the memory of this place, more sweet than pathetic.

Sometime during this same period, for reasons I cannot remember, I became intrigued with the quest narratives, particularly the Arthuriad, which, as far as anyone knows, has its origins in Celtic Brittany. I read as many versions as I could find, even struggling through the Old French. It was an intellectual pursuit at best, however, never a model for my own spiritual journey. The quest was for those taking the high road; my place was lower down among the plebs, those wandering in the wilderness, pilgrims seeking the promised land. In a move that began to reconnect the academic with the spiritual, I wrote a thesis on the wilderness, biblical and literary. It seemed that life was a narrative with a beginning, middle and end – a pilgrimage, you might say – even if at times it came across as an interlocking set of circles stretched out in a line.

The other, more profoundly affecting move occurred when Bob and I took on the restoration of a French village house with all the complexities and strangeness that entailed. Every common task or repair, straightforward in Canada, became momentous and incomprehensible, owing to failures in language and/or technical differences. We congratulated ourselves when the kitchen counters arrived at the right address and miraculously fit the allotted space. We were even more overwhelmed when our neighbours stopped by to chat as we dug in our garden; real understanding of local speech would come later, if at all. Going to the village fête, to the baptism of friends' children, or to a concert in which a friend was singing, were adventures far removed from the ordinary. Although we kept pinching ourselves to make sure that what we were doing wasn't a dream, we began in fact to make a new kind of life here, attempting to adapt and blend in to a milieu in which we felt both outsiders and yet at home. While the inevitable distance being a foreigner creates doesn't necessarily give one the detachment of an Archimedes that permits you to change the world, it does make some difference to how one views oneself. The blurry lines of my wilderness map had stretched over to France.

My first visit in the 1970s to Vézelay in Burgundy instilled in me the love of Romanesque architecture, and sowed the first seeds of the idea of a French pilgrimage. The house we bought sits, whether by good luck or unrecognized design, within easy reach of some of the greatest medieval sites along the famous pilgrimage routes, particularly those leading to the shrine of Santiago de Compostela in northwestern Spain. Some of the Romanesque buildings are still in use, or at least still standing. It was these churches, abbeys, hostels and remnants that I wanted to discover. Besides, since I was already absorbed in medieval romance, it was a quick step from the mystery of the Holy

Grail and its followers to unearthing other medieval narratives – folk tales, poetry of the troubadours, stories about the saints. I decided I would become a pilgrim.

I hoped that my perambulatory research would turn into a book. It was to be art-historical and sociological in focus. This travel book with a difference would be light, humorous, abounding in stories about those devoted, credulous people who lived in the centuries when miracles happened and saints were created with an astonishing frequency. A light, informative book, nothing personal.

From the beginning I felt like a cheat. My peculiar pilgrimage didn't seem to resemble the medieval model at all. The very basic ingredients of a pilgrimage surely required that one headed directly for a particular goal – whether it be Jerusalem, Rome or Compostela – and that one went on foot or on horseback, devoting months to the trip. I wasn't going to do that. Even more basic perhaps than these criteria was the requirement that the pilgrim be a believer – not necessarily a devout one, or a well-meaning one, but one who believed in the efficacy of the trip, that the hardships endured would bring the expected rewards, more or less. In other words, that the saints could help to turn things around in one's life.

From my reading, I discovered that the present understanding of a pilgrimage as a beeline trip to a distant goal arose several hundred years after pilgrimages had begun in Europe, sometime between the ninth and eleventh centuries. Before that, and continuing long afterwards, was the very different idea of "the walk to the saints." The purpose was to meet as many saints as one could, in no particular order, and with no one holy place designated as the ultimate destination, the *sine qua non*…. French historian Raymond Oursel says that medieval people were much more nomadic than we are; they had no sense of home as we know it. People took up residence in foreign places, and travelled about a lot. In the light of this, going to visit the saints was more like a regular ritual than a once-in-a-lifetime event.

This is what I intended to do, setting out in a random way, perhaps even intuitively, to visit cities, shrines and holy places where the saints had lived, worked and been honoured. My travels have been zigzags, circular routes, and broken arcs, returning to our house in Campagnac between sallies. I've visited some of the prescribed stages on the old pilgrimage routes many times, some only once. Persuasively, the American journalist Tony Hiss, in *The Experience of Place*, talks about people needing "a right to roam." Roaming is the way I like to travel: setting off to discover and make use of whatever comes along the way. I need a goal, certainly, but I will follow any byways that show up, and if in the end I don't reach the goal (too much time spent with whatever is fascinating along the side of the road), it doesn't matter. I will be back.

Taken literally, I do not believe in the miraculous abilities of the saints. I find most of the stories medieval people told about the wondrous workings of the saints, whether dead or alive, to be humorous and charming tales – although completely satisfying within a world view that does not draw clear lines between religion, magic, common sense and logic. On the other hand, having been known to step over those lines myself, I believed then, and even more so now, that the interpretation of the remembered history of a particular place or event, the mythology of the saint, one's past experience and present desires, may give rise to a sense of the sacred in the present time. One could call that miraculous.

So right from the start I realized that it wasn't as a usual pilgrim that I wanted to find the saints at their shrines. My goal, after all, was not religious, really. At the time this hesitation made me rather uncomfortable, morally speaking.

I can't call what began to occur in my wanderings a resolution of my discomfort. Rather, what has been coming on during my time of pilgrimage is the sense of an even greater discomfort, of being nudged, prodded and thrown into a tougher wilderness where all choices about roads taken and shrines visited are matters of utter seriousness for my life. Like a dialectical force resolving the opposition between faith and scepticism, personal longings and intellectual detachment, came the shrines themselves. Buildings of persuasive beauty and warm psychological assurance, silent repositories of human stories and deep devotion, they are touchstones. Touchstones resonate with the past and emit power for the present. They have the ability to dispose of all one's problems by their overwhelming statement of what they are, what they have been, and what they will be. They illuminate the way, and like it or not, insist that one must go on.

The book that has emerged took a direction I had never intended. While I had always anticipated sharing my personal theories, ideas and opinions, I wasn't much given to the thought of becoming the main, almost the only character in the narrative. There wasn't much I could do about it, once the stones had begun their work. Either it was this book told in this way, or none at all. Either it was truly *my* pilgrimage, or I was indeed cheating the reader, myself and the sites themselves.

It has turned out that certain of these sites have taken on a kind of symbolic significance, reflecting my ongoing spiritual journey. These are the ones I have chosen to write about, out of the forty or so I have visited. They are also the ones I have returned to more than once, drawing from them each time that *mana* that the Maori say inheres in sacred stones, and hoping to use it well. Of all the touchstones, however, the humble ones that make up our house in Campagnac were the first, and remain the most compelling of all.

In my wanderings I have discovered that medieval people were as worldly as you or I. They had no contempt for lusty pleasures, good food, good stories and jokes, good company, good sex. They were, by and large, not ascetics. Even pilgrims on the long route to Santiago de Compostela, just like Chaucer's motley group, were capable of turning away from their visits to holy places to see the sights, tell droll tales and be rather lax in their behaviour. I do the same. Many wavered between faith and doubt, old pagan beliefs and present orthodoxy, in a way that seems rather familiar to me.

My pilgrimage isn't along dusty roads in broken-down sandals, or sleeping anxiously in fields haunted by fear of storms and wild animals. As I visited the remarkable sites where millions of others have preceded me, or dug in my French garden between journeys, I came to realize how these travels to the saints have both reflected and stimulated the greater pilgrimage which is my life. In turning back to a time when the centre still held, I hoped to learn how our ancestors were able to keep their world together, with all its mysteries, miracles, contradictions and rich emotional stew; and to use that knowledge as one uses wells in the wilderness. This is a record of one pilgrim's thirst, and of some of the wells that have satisfied it.

CHAPTER 1

— CAMPAGNAC —

The casement windows of the small salon are wide open and the ivy has found its way inside the shutters and along the sill. We came late this year, giving it plenty of time to camouflage the whole house, stone walls, weathered shutters and roof tiles, with glistening green. The house looks abandoned again, as it was before we bought it.

We came upon it by accident, although we were on a house-hunting foray at the time. We had been wistfully looking for about ten years, each planned route in France interrupted by little detours, pauses to look excitedly at pathetic, closed-up houses, all abandoned, we thought. (There were usually families living perfectly contentedly behind those closed shutters beside those dreary barnyards.) Finally we decided it was time to call our own bluff: we would spend two weeks in the area we liked best, just looking at houses, and if we didn't find something by then, we'd call the whole thing off.

The region we chose, after much deliberation, is called the Midi-Pyrénées, although the part we had narrowed ourselves down to is neither in the Midi nor the Pyrénées. Lying east of Toulouse and north of Carcassonne, it is a richly endowed area of wooded hills, sloping vineyards and shadowed rivers, little known to outsiders at the time we came upon it, and still today happily free of hordes of people bearing Green Guides, doing their touring by the book. We rented a spot in the area and went out every day with Mlle. Plageoles, a young sociology graduate turned estate agent.

She took us to see all sorts and conditions of houses, mostly those described as *"en mauvais état."* Canadians have no idea what "in poor condition" can mean. We saw houses with fallen beams, stairs so fragile you daren't go up to look at the bedrooms, roofs with tiles sliding off almost as we watched. Once we saw one with plumbing. Our favourite was an old mill composed of two buildings. One could be a bedroom wing, the other used for living. The millstone would have taken up most of what we saw as our living room. The only problem was, the whole vast, beautiful complex lacked a roof. My other favourite, which had an ancient outdoor bake oven – how I fantasized! – would have required, according to Bob and Mademoiselle, removing about half of the house, it was in such *mauvais état*.

Farms were not a good idea, we were told. Friends whose Dutch relatives had a house to sell on the farthest edge of Provence warned us not to think of buying it: the relatives, being absentee owners, had been robbed twice. Buying in a smart area wasn't sensible either, if you intended to be away a lot. My cousins Jack and Clair McCordick told of their neighbours' robbery in Mougins, above Nice: the "repair men" backed a truck up to the door, and emptied the house of everything but the dining room table – it was too large for the doorway. A small, undistinguished village seemed like the best place to settle.

One day wandering around on our own, having exhausted all of Mlle. Plageoles' possibilities, we came upon Campagnac. The village is on the extreme southeastern edge of the department of the Tarn, about an hour's drive from Toulouse. Coming from the nearest town of Gaillac, it is a twenty-minute drive, winding up and down the rounded hills that take up most of this spacious landscape. The land here is a composite of geometrically laid-out fields for grape vines, wheat and cash crops like sunflowers, softened by stands of trees, thick bush and the occasional renovated farmhouse whose showily unproductive flower garden is the sure sign of its gentrification. There is one special curve, just before you start down a hill among overarching trees, where each time I return I catch my breath and let it out with delight. You can see the plain below stretching for miles, small green-blue hills in the near distance; just beneath us is a clear pond filling most of a field, and around it, if we are lucky in our timing, a mass of poppies.

At the intersection that is le Verdier, we are directed to Campagnac, four kilometres away. The road goes through the valley, full of wildflowers, mustard and sunflowers, with patches of slim trees, all deciduous and light. There are very few houses on this road, widely separated, a couple of farmyards with a scattering of chickens. Goodness knows how people here make a living. This is the sort of valley about which poems are written, pastoral but impractical.

Finally, among row upon row of burgeoning vines, some gnarled and firmly upright, others newly planted, their leaves delicate and tentative, the road winds up the hill, a group of buildings appears on the horizon – crowned by the church steeple and the fortress-like château – and you arrive in Campagnac.

On this momentous day, Bob and I stopped in the village square to have a quick lunch in the car. Across the road was what looked like a typical old eyesore of a stuccoed house, the kind we'd been seeing in every down-on-its-uppers rural community. The front wall directly abutting the street was covered with fragments of old posters and notices, and one notice way up high that said *À vendre*. Through the rusty iron gate you could see weeds as high as a *chèvre*'s eye all the way to the front door. Bushwhacking our way there we found the door unlocked, went inside and opened every shutter in the house. A quick look at the rooms, with their beautiful proportions, and at the view decided us: it was going to be ours. Within a week it was so.

It didn't have everything. Built with solid stone walls, it has a fine new tile roof, a low stone wall around the garden, a marvellous view of vineyards and the hills beyond. Inside it has six fireplaces, windows everywhere, many large rooms with three-metre-high ceilings. It didn't have plumbing or usable electricity, and virtually all the walls needed re-plastering. The kitchen was bare, except for a hole in the outside wall where water could run out from whatever had passed for a sink, now missing. Encroaching tree roots had caused one corner of the house to crack and gape widely. The main floor was – and still is – tile laid directly on beaten earth. Upstairs the wooden floors were full of woodworm, a common enough complaint, but it looked risky.

We could see that it had once been a house of some dignity. The wallpapers on every room, browned and mouldy, had been very handsome, of the eighteenth-century brocaded roses sort, with touches of gilt. The living room has a lovely plaster medallion with a design of bunches of grapes, from which an oil lamp would have hung on a hook. The fireplace in the smaller salon has a faux-neoclassical surround, and five of the six fireplaces are marble.

Outdoors, the garden had been taken over by nettles, creeping everybody, and one muscular weed we called the Queen Mum, because it looked like Queen Anne's Lace, but was older and stronger. Miraculously, the fieldstone wall that held back these aggressive interlopers was still almost entirely intact. The well in the perfect centre of this wilderness held water, though its pump was disabled.

That first autumn we spent our holiday stripping wallpapers, and getting ready for the plasterer, the plumber, the electrician and the septic tank-er, all ably coordinated by Tom Butcher, an expatriate Englishman specializing in restoration work. The following spring we began the decorative work – painting, staining, de-woodworming, tiling – with the help of our son Andrew and a girlfriend unhappily pressed into service. It didn't seem like work, these jobs that I'd never think of doing at home. It's not monotonous when everything you touch is different. The paint coated weirdly, and sometimes not at all. Some of the wallpaper refused to come off until heroic measures were taken. It was a lark, spraying the floors for woodworm, and then going away overnight to a little auberge until the smell disappeared. I've never felt more creative than while bringing this trusty dowager back to life. Obviously there was much more at stake here than simply doing house renovations. Fifteen years later, while we continue to lavish it with comforts and treasures, it has everything we actually need, except central heat, and to afford that we'll have to win a lottery.

I've always wanted to live in a stone house. Stone has a resolute dignity, a subtle beauty in the faintly shifting tonalities of each block, whether it has been cut or dragged out of the ground. Even the discolorations that accrue to old monuments or buildings do not override the complex character of the material itself. Our modernist house in St. Catharines has several important stone walls making both sense and statement: they house fireplaces and "protect" the other wooden walls beside them. The two houses are quite dissimilar in mood and in sense of space. The St. Catharines house is full of clutter, signs of work, hobbies and decorative acquisitions. Objects appear and sometimes disappear on every surface: tables, chairs, walls, floors. Plants jostle for space with the animals, three very furry cats and a Bouvier. Family jokes are made about the need for another addition made up entirely of cupboards and bookshelves, or, better still, a garage sale. The Campagnac house developed its character from another impetus, and with fewer needs. It is spacious, white and simple, and will probably stay that way, except for the music tapes and books that come over by the suitcase-load. It is the house of ease, of promise, of otherness. Unlike its opposite number, it has so far been blithely free of seasons of pervasive gloom, attacks of mid-life anxiety, build-ups of angry disputing, tears of loss to which I am sometimes subject. It misses too the peaks of excitement that crown those demanding enterprises that have taken so long to succeed. Most of all, it waits, like a scarcely marked sheet of white paper, for the reunion of our whole family here. So far our children have each come once, and not all together. I can hardly wait till it happens: that will be some excitement.

Then there was the garden to deal with, or what we thought might have been one. It was impossible to tell at first. Over the years Bob and I converted this tough terrain ourselves, by use of fork and spade, to grass and shrubs, ringed by madame the former owner's lovely acacia, lilacs and fruit trees, and her long-lost lilies, iris, yucca and roses. An inauthentic electric pump was lowered into the well to help supply water for the garden. The result of our efforts won't make the garden glossies still, but to us it is Edenic.

We call the house "Colomba." For several years we thought and thought about a name, and couldn't come up with anything. Finally I found a lovely tile in Portugal, and wanting someplace special for it, decided to put it on the outside wall beside the front door. It has three white doves on it. *"Les Colombes"* sounded about as corny for a French house name as it would be in English, but recalling how captivated I had been at university by Mérimée's *Colomba*, a novel about a fierce Corsican heroine, I decided that variant would be more impressive. A bird-watching visitor says that the proper name of the pigeons who live here, there, and all over the village, is *Columba Livia*. So now we have a polyvalent symbol: it can refer to dirty birds, a strong woman with violence on her mind, or – they're doves, after all – the Holy Spirit. All this from a Portuguese souvenir!

Change of ownership in France doesn't include a title search; there was therefore no easy way to date the house. I felt as though I was in a historical limbo. I wanted to be linked up to the broader current of events: to find out whether we were launched as a consequence of some larger socio-economic plan; whether we were pre-war or post-war, and if so, which war. I wanted to know why this house is different from any other house in the village: more pretentious although no larger than the rest, with hints of a more recent reno – the plaster ceiling medallion and the mantelpieces – but how recent?

Our neighbours in the château opposite, the Nohens, had one explanation. They thought the house had belonged to the farm manager for the château. Since the latter was constructed over a period of about two hundred years, ending in the sixteenth century, this wasn't a lot of help, especially since our house is clearly much newer than that. As you'd expect, even long-time village residents had no idea of its age. "I think it must be about a hundred," I said. "Oh, much older!" they all said. I guess we'll never know whether Napoleon's equerries slept here.

We were just as mystified when we tried to find out about the people who had lived here in the recent past. Somewhere in the telling of it I detect a myth creeping in on little furry feet, leaving hints of itself in the corners, in the garden and on the windowsills: yes, especially on the windowsills. Here's what I know:

We bought the house from a doctor and his wife who live in Paris, and who had owned it for ten years. I can't imagine why they bought it, because his wife hated the country and the south, and she never came here. The doctor came a couple of times, and had the good sense to put on a new roof. Other than that nothing was done, inside or out.

We inherited therefore the vestiges of living left us by the previous owner once removed. Looking at the shells and discards we wondered about the people who, in 1975, would have lived this way, in rooms with touches of elegance almost overriding the patches of peasantry, and yet without plumbing or sanitation. So far I have been given two answers to my questions; as to which, if either, is the autho-rized version, I cannot decide.

Madame Bonnet, the long-time mayor's wife, tells me that it was an elderly widow who lived here. She and her husband lived on a farm just north of the village, on the road to Vaour, and when he died she came to live in this house. It was very sad, her death: she was leaning out of the upstairs hall window to feed the birds, the sill was icy, and she fell.

Anna and Arnold Cragg, from London, have had a *maison secondaire* not quite in Campagnac but in Frescal, about 300 metres away from us, for twenty-odd years. Anna, who works in the theatre, and could be forgiven for enhancing a biography somewhat, remembers Madame. She visited her often, in her salon crowded with pictures and mementos. She had been a hat couturier in Paris, had retired here – I don't remember any mention of a husband – and had found few people of like interests. Depressed, one winter's day she threw herself out of the upstairs hall window. Anna was not surprised.

I'm tempted to leave well enough alone, and let the two stories float where they will. But logic prevails over mythopoeia, and the search for the true version goes on. In the first place, the windowsills come up to my waist, and Madame I was told was much shorter than I. How could she have slipped over the sill? Feeding birds from the upper storey seems a bit peculiar since there are no branches near enough even to hang balls of suet.

Digging in the garden we discovered a midden quite close to the house, and in it, among other things, were many glass portions of syringes of the sort used by diabetics. Could it be that the explanation is neither of the above stories, but something more brutally banal? Could she have passed out and fallen? So far, no ghost has turned up to give me the straight goods.

The midden, by the way, yielded, besides the usual crockery bits and the odd teaspoon, about two hundred small metal stampings shaped like horseshoes. These are the cleats that cobblers put on the heels and toes of boots to prevent wear. Now I can't imagine Madame as the village boot maker, so possibly here is the first hint of an even earlier owner who carried out his trade in our vast cave. Every year the garden gives up more artifacts, but so far nothing from the Roman occupation, nor the Visigoths.

The square is the only example of town planning in the village. There isn't much more to the village, actually. Pilar Noya, our beloved house minder, tells me there are twenty-eight families here, but I know that's in Greater Campagnac, the commune. The core has half that many. At one end of the square is the *mairie*, with its perpetually mis-curled flag wound limply over the pole. The château borders on the square, as does the church. At the other end, beside a row of chestnut trees, is a typical, ugly crucifix about 3.5 metres high. Hedging its bets, I'm sure the agnostic village will never take it down. Even the pigeons don't like it.

Most squares at one time or another will have a bevy of bereted men of middle age or beyond, playing *boules*, with a few children on the sidelines. (Once I saw a woman playing. I'd love to know how she beat that unwritten men-only law.) The only sport I've ever seen here is when my young cousin from Paris, Alexis from the château and Vincent, the Deleportes' son, used to get on their bikes and rally round the square. They're too old for that now, so it's pretty dormant over there.

The fantasy-making part of me would like to upgrade our square, filling it with a humming market once a week, bright, overflowing flowerpots around the *mairie*, perhaps a small fountain or at least a well. I would like it to look like all those quaint squares that get photographed for calendars, showing the two *vieillards* chatting on a bench beside a wisteria-drenched wall, a drowsy black and white no-breed dog at their feet. The other part of me says no, leave things as they are, neither prettified nor sentimentalized. This is your France, not the film-set version.

Twice a day, at noon and 7:30 p.m., the bells in the church tower ring the Angelus. I look over in the square where a few people are standing conversing. Nobody stops talking. For a long time I wondered why the little church would continue to peal out its call to prayer when no one prayed. Then I realized that here the Angelus only signifies quitting time. As a dinner bell it couldn't be bettered. There is no sound quite like the Campagnac bell. Its rhythm is almost but not quite syncopated, making its two notes unforgettable. Andrew, who composes music, was so intrigued that he wrote a piece called "The Bells of Campagnac." One day it should be a great hit.

When I was growing up we used to hear church bells from every steeple in our town. Now there are fewer and they seem weaker to me. In France every village seems to have one. Some of them are perhaps old enough to have tolled in pilgrims' ears. Monasteries in remote places such as Aubrac to the north of us used to sound their bells all night to guide lost pilgrims. That must have ruffled the composure of a few monks, for they had little enough sleep as it was.

Ever since we've been in Campagnac the church has been closed. Those who do so must worship at Castelnau-de-Montmiral, ten minutes away. Still, it's a trim little stone building with clean-cut buttresses, its neighbours the mayor's gigantic tractor in the attached open shed, and the electrician's van on its verge. Without them it would be quite desolate. The church is dedicated to St. Eusèbe, but since there were three saints of that name, all of whom died, strangely enough, in the fourth century, I guess we'll never know our local luminary's particular attributes, nor how he looks after us. The upper part of the church has been completely rebuilt – it has 1636 carved over the door – but when it was originally built is not known, at least to the writer of the little local history book I found. In 1946 it became one of two points to be served by the same *curé*, the other being Le Verdier four kilometres away. Now it is left friendless.

I saw the inside of the church once, when it was opened for a special occasion. Jean-Claude and Michèle Nohen, Parisians who use their château as a *maison secondaire*, decided to have their children baptized there, got in the priest from Castelnau, and invited the whole village to come. It was a warm-hearted family day. The priest took charge of the village as all of us assembled in the square. He welcomed us to the baptism, and said a lot of other meaningful things I couldn't quite understand, but I knew that I was, like everyone else there, a participant in bringing these children into the New Life. So we went inside this damp, undernourished place, and did it; Jean-Claude read a lesson, the priest got us all singing the refrain of a folky hymn, and the children were baptized. Then everyone went back out into the square, chatted away for a bit, and went home until five o'clock when the feasting part began in the château.

This is no fancy Loire château with needle-sharp towers, moat and Renaissance maze-like gardens. This one consists of one round tower at the end, abutting an 18-metre-long rectangle. No moat, and the small garden is planned around children, bikes, a ping-pong table and a pint-sized swimming pool. Still it is a tough, handsome building, some of whose parts have been around for six hundred years. "We bought it for the staircase," Jean-Claude says, which spirals up inside the tower. Going up the stone steps you are transported to the time of the Lady of Shalott, or Iseult headed for a tryst. The date is carved under a stair: 1548.

Almost every day you can see the Campagnac Air Force on the roof of the château. Andrew named them: they're the pigeons who form up each day along the ridgepole. They gather in a single line, then a small flight will go off on manoeuvres or on a recce, and come back into formation to report. We haven't seen much of them recently. They're a dirty, noisy lot, even when on duty, so perhaps Jean-Claude has found ways of dealing with them. Still it was nice to think we had local protection of some sort.

They're back again today, practising boomerang manoeuvres: the leader gives a hoarse command, then a platoon sweeps off the roof ridge, does a swift circle and comes back again in twenty seconds. End of practice. Dismiss.

The rest of the village spreads out from the square. There are no new houses; the empty house across from us has 1860 carved over the door, and from the look of things, that was the last period of building construction here. When the grape harvest, the *vendange*, is taking place, we see a lot of young new faces on the gargantuan tractors that pass through to dump their lees behind the *mairie*. Otherwise the only traffic coming down our road, besides a few locals from Vaour, is the excursion buses taking "the grannies," as Tom calls them, out for a day in the country.

The drowsy little Campagnac of today was apparently not so peaceful in earlier times. Its most eventful epoch was the sixteenth century, during the Wars of Religion. Campagnac went Protestant and as a result suffered from the comings and goings of freedom allotted to the reformed religion by ever-changing royal moods. At one point the Catholics decided to burn the village, but a truce was achieved and it was spared. There was a Protestant temple or church here between 1568 and 1679, but where it might be found I don't know. When the Protestant viscount of Poulin wanted to build a house, he was given permission as long as it was indefensible. He disobeyed and raised a strong château. After threats to dismantle it were waived, and agreements drawn up, it was finally completed at the end of the sixteenth century. This is the château now owned by the Nohens.

How tantalizing these little bits of local history are! It is amazing that such an insignificant place should have any records at all, I suppose. The population register shows that in 1836 Campagnac had an all-time high of 447 people. Where are the buildings they used now? Reformed into walls and fences? Buried under the soil? It has made a slow but certain descent, until 1982 when this booklet was written, and there were 113 persons living here. Today Annie-France Emmery tells me there are 86 on the voting list, so perhaps we are on the upswing again. Since I began writing this, three new families with children have moved in, and the long-empty house on the square has just been rented to a couple who are French but from away.

Being a stranger to this village, this region, this country, I would like to make connections with the past, find the invisible history, put down some tender roots. So I grasp at fabled connections, such as this one: The census of 1885 gives the names of the professions practised by the villagers. They are by now all tradespeople – no more doctors, lawyers or judges, as in earlier times. There are two shoemakers listed, named Bayles and Taillefer. In the light of our find of metal cleats in the midden, perhaps one of them lived here. I think Taillefer may be an earlier version of the name Teilhefer, and hence an old family. I will ask Mlle. Teilhefer, who lives up the hill in Beaudinencq, if her family ever lived in this house.

My father's family, the McCordicks, are thought to be Huguenots whose name before they went to Ireland was Cardiac. It occurred to me that it would be amusing for a tanner's daughter (me) to have bought a shoemaker's house, for a Cardiac to have come to Campagnac.

Today my neighbours seem so thoroughly grounded in their homes, their social life and their occupations – so very different from my own situation. It astonishes me to see that their families have been here for more than two hundred years – and I wonder for how much longer. Jean Coursières was consul in 1758; we buy wine in Graddé from his descendant. Mlle. Teilhefer's roots go back to the mid-seventeenth century: her ancestor was a consul. Mme. Molinier's and M. Molinier's families are both on the 1801 census, as is M. Poussou's, whose winery is just below us. M. Bonnet's and our new mayor Alain Maroulle's families' names appear on the parish register between 1640 and 1660. The records also show that M. Bonnet, who was mayor when we first came, had been so for thirty years, the longest reign of any mayor here.

Just the fact that you are a Canadian means that you have been uprooted at least once. Although my family is old by New World standards – five generations on my father's side and many more on my mother's have lived in North America – it is not the same as having lived on and by the land for uncounted centuries, knowing no other way of life. Besides, the members of my family that I have always been most attracted to are the uprooted ones – Doris and Hubert, my Italian cousins who live in Paris, my diplomatic cousins who have lived in so many places. What I always thought was the bonding material among us – love of music, art and literature – may be just one part of the amalgam. It may be that a stronger and deeper sense is interfused. Call it the search for another perspective, the desire to connect past and present, I don't know. In my case, you could call it the pilgrim spirit. Historian Colin Morris, talking about the disruptive effect of conflicting values in the twelfth century, says, "In one form or another, the problem of alienation and order was central in the literature of the twelfth century, and the sense of alienation was expressed in one of the most powerful symbols which have been devised for it: pilgrimage." There is the first connection between these medieval people and me. Others no doubt will follow.

I now know that "Colomba" is the first stage on my French pilgrimage. To begin with, it has a warming effect on my religious imagination: I have come to agree wholeheartedly with Browning's Fra Lippo Lippi who said that the world "means intensely, and means good" – or at least it should, and here it does so. Also, it brings together the far and near and jangles them about a lot. My Canadian religious searchings meet the French countryside and its inhabitants. My recently liberated feminist theological leanings come up against present and historical French piety.

Leaving "Colomba" on my way to the saints, I am attempting to make some trails through my twentieth-century wilderness by following some revered, dusty ones. In the hope of bringing the mind to its senses, I go to search out some touchstones, stones still imbued with the *mana* invested in them by the saints and those who visited them. In the end, though, my reason for going is the same as St. Augustine's, who said: Keep going along the road, never satisfied. If you stop, you die.

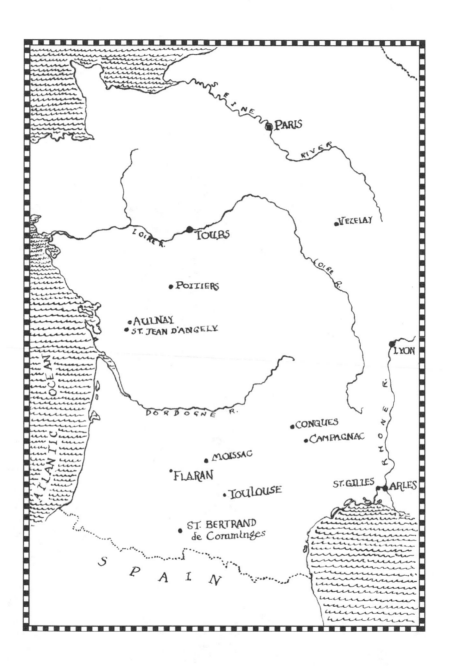

CHAPTER 2

— VÉZELAY—

Magdala, Mary of. *Saint. b? Palestine?; d? Sainte-Baume, France? Described by the Evangelists as a sinner, forgiven by Jesus. One of the women who waited at Calvary during the Crucifixion. First person to speak to Jesus after his Resurrection. Often portrayed with long hair and fine clothing, barefoot, holding a silver jar or* coffret.

Over the centuries, Vézelay has launched hundreds of thousands on new journeys of faith. It launched me.

In the Middle Ages if you wanted to go on a long and spiritually rewarding pilgrimage full-time, you had three choices of destination: Jerusalem, Rome or Santiago de Compostela. Pilgrimages to Santiago de Compostela began late in the ninth century, after the discovery of the bones of St. James buried in a field in this furthest northwestern corner of Spain. One legend says that a peasant was guided by a star to their location: hence the name Compostela, or field of the star. The more conventional report is that the bishop of a neighbouring city found them. Whoever was responsible, the find turned out to be one of the greatest treasures of the Christian world.

There is very little in the Bible about James, one of the famous triumvirate of disciples closest to Jesus. In the gospels he remains in the shadow of the other two, Peter and John. To the early Christians he was very important, however, since he headed the young Christian community in Jerusalem. James' approach to living sounds like the monastic ascetic ideal. Eusebius, the first Christian historian, says that James drank no wine or alcohol, ate nothing that tasted pleasant, never oiled his body nor took baths. "The skin of his knees was like a camel's, for he was constantly prostrating himself before God in adoration, and to ask pardon for his people." He was beheaded by the Romans in AD 44.

The first known biography of James appeared in the south of France, and from the sixth century on the stories about him grew. About the same time the belief arose that the known world had been divided up among the apostles, and James had been given Spain. Quite appropriately, James' body had been brought there by his followers after his untimely death.

In the ninth century two things happened that changed the image of the apostle radically and gave him contemporary prominence. It was told that in 844 at the battle of Clavijo, James appeared as an armoured warrior brandishing a sword and a white standard with a red cross, enabling the Spaniards to defeat the Moors, and earning him the title *Santiago Matamoros*, slayer of Moors. At almost the same time, whether coincidentally or not, Bishop Théodemir (d. 847) found the body of the saint at Compostela. A mausoleum was built, then a larger one. By the end of the century, pilgrimages had begun, and within fifty years there are records of bishops, an archbishop and other notables who went to what at the time must have seemed the end of the earth to venerate the saint's remains.

St. James' shrine was so enthusiastically visited because it contained the whole body of the saint. In an era when relics (i.e., parts) of saints were lost, stolen or sold, James was one of the rarities, as this twelfth-century writer says effulgently:

That the body is immovable is well known from the testimony of Théodomir, Bishop of this city, who found it in time past, and was unable to stir it from its place. So let the folk beyond the mountains blush when they claim to have any part of it, or relics of him.

The cathedral, which had been burnt, rebuilt and enlarged, was finally gloriously completed in the early thirteenth century. This was its heyday. Much later, pilgrimages fell off, the relics were lost for three hundred years, found again and declared authentic by the pope in the nineteenth century. The wave of pilgrims started up again. In our time two million pilgrims visit the shrine in jubilee years, when his feast day, July 25, falls on a Sunday.

Vézelay is one of the gathering places, celebrated starting points for one of the four main pilgrimage routes through France to Santiago de Compostela. On a trip as daunting as this, it was essential to travel in groups for safety's sake. For a long time after the Christian re-conquest of Spain, both France and Spain were still very unsettled and pilgrims were easy prey for human and animal predators. You needed all the help you could get. Companionship and mutual protection were essential. So pilgrims coming from the north would gather in

Paris, Orléans or Tours; coming from northeastern Europe, they would meet at Vézelay; from the east, at le Puy; and from the south, on what was known as "The Italian Road," they would gather at Arles. There were many other less travelled routes; pilgrims would visit as many saints as dwelt on or close to the road between home and the nearest major route. Every year I watch the proliferation of signs at the entrance to medieval towns which say, "Stage on the route to Santiago de Compostela."

April is the month when Chaucer's pilgrims "longen to goon on pilgrimage," but for the McPhersons it is May. I'd guess that out of about forty-five trips to France, thirty of them have been in May. I can't remember when I first heard of Vézelay, or what led me to it, but we came there first in May 1972 on our third trip to France. I believe we were on our way to taste the great wines of Burgundy, which we had drunk often enough at home in those plummy days when the difference between an ordinary Graves and a Montrachet – ah, Montrachet! – was a dollar fifty. I remember that we came up to it from the east, along the dusky, wooded river valley where we had spent the previous night in a converted mill, listening to nothing but trees and flowing water. In retrospect, such a soothing vigil couldn't be bettered as preparation for the shock of the next day.

It doesn't hit you all at once. First there is the long straight road for a couple of kilometres or so through open fields, at the end of which the village (population 571) circles a prominent hill like a diadem, basking in the homage of the lesser treed slopes around it. Closer in, Vézelay looks more like a jumble of structural efforts, the highest of which is a towered building that seems churchlike but, well, different. Then you lose sight of it as you make a slow, curving ascent up the hill through veils of palest green leaves on an early spring afternoon. It really isn't until you have negotiated the winding cobbled streets to the top and walked into the plaza in front of the basilica that you know you have arrived.

The basilica of Saint Mary Magdalene, called the Madeleine, takes up only one side of the square, but its presence is so imposing everything else escapes notice. It is like no building I have ever seen, with a tall tympanum shaped more like a hoop than a half-moon. (I had seen pictures of these Romanesque constructs, imposing curved spaces above the main doors that are filled with carved stone figures, and so I knew what it should look like.) With only one tower, though, it is lopsided, and even my untrained eye can tell it is no purely Romanesque design. I can glimpse the rest of the church stretching out behind the façade, curving lines in stone going on forever it seems. This is the genuine article, I decide: how was I supposed to know that the whole building had had a massive restoration in the nineteenth century? I doubt it would have spoiled the moment had I known.

From every aspect I am astonished, thrown off balance by this imperiously captivating structure. Trying to recall what it was I thought more than twenty-five years ago, it was, I believe, the impossibility of it all. I was standing in front of the same doors that had opened for thousands, perhaps millions of other pilgrims, seekers, voyeurs for nine hundred years. It was the sense of connectedness between me and those unknown people, made almost physical by the church's presence. History wasn't a subject of study; history included me, today, and all the rest in their time.

Charles Williams, the English mystic, writer and friend of Tolkien and C.S. Lewis, part of that literary circle who called themselves The Inklings, was my author of choice in those days. He, of all people, would have understood what I felt in the square before the Madeleine of Vézelay. Time, he might have said, is a human construct; from the divine point of view, all time is the present, and therefore connections between historical moments and our own time are real connections. It is God's way of making it possible to bring all lapsed, uncaring lives into the great plan of creation-salvation.

Attempting to take in the Christian story that is Vézelay, I had a glimpse of what Williams was on about, though it is as unfathomable as any other great religious understanding. So many significant events have taken place here. On the slopes of this hill in 1147, St. Bernard of Clairvaux called the faithful to join the Second Crusade. Sitting beside him ready to lead them was Louis VII of France and his queen-for-a-time, Eleanor of Aquitaine. The atmosphere must have sparkled with the force of dedication to serve under the cross and – let's not be blind to motivations – the urge to escape from the banal regularity of everyday life, a keenness for adventure, and hatred of the infidels who trampled the holy shrines. The Madeleine has been the site of other notable occurrences, such as its dedication by Pope Innocent II, and – one in which admirers of T.S. Eliot still rejoice – the excommunication of Henry II's closest advisers by his archbishop Thomas à Becket. The Third Crusade began from here too, led by the heroic but failed crusader Richard the Lion Heart, imprisoned in Austria on his way home, and ransomed at a staggering cost by his devoted mother the dauntless Eleanor.

What brought them all here in the first place was the bones. It was on a feast day in 1037 that the abbot of the Benedictine monastery showed the world for the first time the relics of St. Mary Magdalene, which were in their keeping. While this may have been a deliberate publicity ploy on someone's part, at the same time both monks and pilgrims were convinced of the genuineness of the relics. The great basilica was begun in 1096 in order to receive the visitors who arrived in droves.

The whole story behind the appearance of the bones is dubious, but of course no one can say whether it was even somewhat factual, or completely concocted by enemies of the newly rich and important site. It is told that Mary Magdalene, together with Martha, Lazarus and two other Marys, were put out to sea, in a boat without sail or oars, by "the heathens" to punish them for being associated with Jesus. They landed on the Mediterranean coast of France. Mary Magdalene, after spending thirty years as a hermit in a cave, died and was buried there. Much later, during the trash-and-burn Arab invasions of the south, a monk from Vézelay was sent to rescue the saint's relics from the monastery church of Saint-Maximin near Marseille where they were kept. Saint-Maximin says they were stolen, but safekeeping is a rationalization that's hard to combat. In consequence, Vézelay became one of the main gathering points, not only for the Crusades but also for one of the pilgrimage routes to Santiago de Compostela. Venerating these efficacious bones would have been a superlative send-off for such gruelling enterprises. In 1279, however, everything changed. The monks of Saint-Maximin, who claimed to have found again the entire corpus of Mary Magdalene, were confirmed in their opinion by Pope Boniface VIII. The path to Vézelay became over-grown with weeds.

If one thinks about it now with the kind of reasonable unreason that I'm sure the monks were capable of as well as I, it doesn't make sense not to have accepted both sets of relics. After all, the medieval figure of the saint Mary Magdalene was a composite of four different biblical and post-biblical Marys and other unidentified women, as all those scholarly religious probably knew. In addition to the woman named Mary Magdalene in the gospels, who was present at the Crucifixion and the Resurrection of Jesus, there was Mary of Bethany, sister of Martha and Lazarus; the prostitute who washed Jesus' feet with tears; the woman who anointed him with precious perfume; and a later repentant prostitute called Mary the Egyptian. So, why not deconstruct the saint, so to speak, and attach the bones to the appropriate Marys? Everyone wins. While this sounds cynical, it wouldn't have been then – just a good idea that no one thought of in time. Unfortunately, long before relic collecting became an absorbing passion, Pope Gregory the Great had made things difficult: he declared that the Marys and the other women of the different gospel episodes were actually one and the same person.

As I realize now, the Madeleine was an utterly astonishing introduction to Romanesque architecture, with its hilltop eminence, the rich sobriety of the whole structure, and the remarkable sculpture. The oddball façade is nothing compared to what you see when you go inside into the porch. A massive, carved tympanum dominates the inner doorway separating the porch from the church. Supporting it and bisecting the two doors of the entrance is a pillar, or *trumeau*, on which a life-size John the Baptist stands. Your eyes go right up to the tympanum itself, glorious theology enacted in stone. For its central scene, the three hemicircles arching over it, and a frieze of small, lively figures below, all illustrate the grand idea that is the Pentecost event: the gift of the powerful Spirit of God. The focal point is the hieratic figure of Christ, twice the size of the surrounding disciples and of me, his head breaking through the hemicircle of figures above. He spreads out his arms over the disciples to point them to the world they are being sent to evangelize: that is the reason they have been given the Holy Spirit. Potential converts, like the Ethiopians and Armenians, appear in the first hemicircle, and in the frieze are some fantastic figures invented by the sculptor. The next hemicircle has homely scenes representing the Zodiac, giving the carver a chance to include all sorts of people working at their humble best.

The work is brilliant, the concept admirable. Here is the hope of salvation being offered to the whole world. Christ is no stiff, remote, iconic figure. The way he is carved sitting sideways, the lines of his robe almost in motion, I know this is a real hope because he is involved, doing his part, in charge. He holds out the possibility that everyone has a chance to succeed. How modern this multicultural vision is; it is too bad that as we enter this new millennium we haven't caught up with it yet. We are still under the impression that to be in the salvation club you must play by certain rules, repeat certain formulae, follow specific procedures. Rules that some people will just never learn.

The tympanum towers over the spacious porch, the un-consecrated part of the church built especially for pilgrims who wanted to spend the night either in vigil or asleep. The monks put down straw for the guests, roused them early and swept out the place before the first services took place. Sounds very much like youth hostels today. I wonder if pilgrims invented the first sleeping bags.

After the dimly pious interiors of the churches I had been used to, with their mean, condescending stained-glass windows, the bright, soaring interior of the basilica seems like a wholly new statement about a lively religion. Everything is suddenly simplified. Here in this building is the Christian experience in faith, and in truth. The only possible response for me to such a statement is: Of course! Annihilating, at least for a time, all my hesitations and arguments about this absurd, demanding religion, I have a glimpse of how the world is to be known and loved. The building shows the way. The shape of the basilica, modelled on the rectangular Roman court of law to represent the earth with a rounded apse at the end signifying heaven, is unsullied. The long line of pillars in the nave draws you up; the round vault, with transverse arches in alternating cream and putty-coloured stone, stops you from flying off and brings you back again. This harmony of poise and balance reminds me how we too have come to be over time: we defy the law of gravity by standing upright. Grounded, but stretching: pillars, arches and people.

Yet all is not regular, pristine and perfect, as it seems at first. The stone is mottled, variegated; only in the vaults is the tone the same.

On the columns, piers and walls, the different coloured stones are placed irregularly, which is not surprising when you are building walls of such varied material, but even the height of the stones on each column is different. This is the wanton, world-affirming attractiveness of the body of the basilica, the Romanesque part: in the Gothic apse all is white and regular, just as I suppose heaven is meant to be.

Architectural critics are vocal about the mistaken, overdone restoration of the Madeleine undertaken by the young architect Viollet-le-Duc in the nineteenth century. Without him it would likely have disintegrated, say its defendants. For the modern pilgrim it is a chance to see a Romanesque building breathing lightly the way it did when it was new.

On one visit we stood beside an English-speaking tourist who was reading the history of the building. Obviously this was his first Romanesque building, too, because all he could say was, "1104! Jesus Christ!"

The basilica changed my brand of piety, probably for the better. I suppose I could say that I moved from an exclusive way of devotion to the inclusive. At home, a regular churchgoer, I loved to belt out the hymns along with an enthusiastic congregation, but for the rest of the service I wanted to be on my own. Alone in my little prayer shell, I shut out the others, and made my bid for God's attention. Of course I knew He was listening and responding to the others too, but each of us had our own special line, something like talking in a row of telephone booths, and I wasn't too interested in what the rest of the collectivity was thinking or hoping for. The most suitable environment for this kind of cubicle-based prayer was a dark one: a Victorian church with the rare shot of divine light coming through the old stained glass. A pew to one-self was best, and if the church was High Anglican enough, the smell of incense could rise up with one's prayer, as one of the psalms says it does. In such a place prayer became rich, intense, full of sentiment and possibly even fruitful: who can say?

Vézelay is bright and beautiful, full of laughter, which is a communal activity, and wonder, which is best when shared. If I were alone in this powerful church, I might feel lonely, perhaps even disoriented. I don't know; I've always been there among plenty of people. It is a church for a community, not for maverick souls. I suppose it is the fact that the light streams in equally on everyone, at the sun's discretion, that made me want to come out of my superiority hermitage and be with the faithful and the sceptical and the rest of the tourists. Then gradually it came to penetrate my spiritual understanding that God is a god of this world, too, in all its loveliness and ugliness, not solely of the mystical other-where. Although none of the awe and majesty was stripped away, God was all the same involved with the whole funny lot of us. That's the other half of the tympanum's message. Vézelay is living proof.

Now that the sun has gone under, the whiteness inside is cool, like a divinity without flesh and blood. I go to find the presence of woman.

At first it appears that there is little to indicate that this is the church of Mary Magdalene. The crypt below the crossing holds one small relic (unspecified) which formerly belonged to the monks of the abbey of Sens. The rest of the body disappeared during the Protestant wars of the sixteenth century. That's what the sign in the church says. The precious, last-remaining relic resides in a graceful glass casket supported by two gilded angels and four other notables – bishops or saints. The womblike, groin-vaulted crypt can hold a dozen devotees comfortably, and although it is so low it doesn't seem claustrophobic, probably because there were no suffocating lit candles.

Although the relic is out of fashion – only one person came and sat in the crypt while I stayed there – the saint is popular here. In one of the transepts stands an ugly, unsuitable marble figure dated 1923. She is holding the traditional jar of ointment with which Mary Magdalene is supposed to have anointed Jesus as a sign of his death and burial to come. On this latest visit, an ordinary day, crowds of women, literal-ly, are lining up to pay their 5 or 10 francs for a short or tall candle, and then trying to find spaces for their lit offerings on the candle stands. There are none. I decide I will make my prayer/meditative request at some other shrine, even though that disrupts the great chain of hagiological being. I can hardly carry my candle around the church with me singing "Jesus bids us shine."

The people lighting up were all *troisième âge* (such a gentle way of saying senior citizens), dusty, plainly dressed, bespectacled and unmade-up. If they bore any resemblance to Mary the redheaded, sup-posedly seductive sinner, it was long gone. I wonder why they admire her: is it because she is penitent? faithful? a good friend? And what sort of prayers does she answer today? I'd love to have been able to ask, but it would have been impertinent. I think these utterly traditional-seeming women would tell a different story than I would about the four-in-one Mary.

On my first and several subsequent visits I certainly held no unorthodox views about her; rather I found her story exotic and intriguing, especially her friendship with Jesus, in which there seemed to be a meeting of minds that he shared with her and no one else. That was the part of the compiled biography I chose to think about. No suspicion of my later heretical views crossed my mind: namely, that for the qualities I overlooked – her sexual misdemeanours, repentance, and tearful, submissive behaviour – she was a poor role model impressed upon women to make them feel guilty and shove them into a forced repentance for actions that usually weren't sinful at all. (No, I am not advocating liberal hookerdom.) I didn't know then that the celibate, scholarly monks were writing – out of their vast experience of marriage! – that women were born lustful, incapable of taming their own urges, and therefore had to be kept under control by their husbands and by penitential duties. The woman called in the gospels simply "a sinner" (part of the Mary Magdalene figure) was automatically taken to be an adulteress: she had to be, women were like that. This was the legacy of Eve. Mary Magdalene's claim to superiority over other women lay in the depth of her contrition and her faith. What was so admirable about her, these men said, was her humility, and the fact that she was persistent in her love for Jesus. (Elaine Pagels says she was venerated because she gave up sex.) The monks believed that these qualities were acquired, not natural. So Mary Magdalene was humble, obedient and controlled, overcoming her lust. Eve, on the other hand, was proud, disobedient and of course oversexed. The odious comparison between the two women was constantly made, and has persisted ever since. Eve did us in: Mary Magdalene can help to save us. No wonder the received images of these two women have been targets of feminist theological attack. They underlie so much that is wrong with societal and ecclesiastical thinking about women.

One of my earliest problems with the church's view of women is that I could not – and still cannot – see humility, obedience and repression of desire as virtues, and their opposites as vices. Humility when taken as proper self-esteem I do certainly subscribe to; but it never means that to the pious. Instead it means putting yourself down unnecessarily, disclaiming any virtues or excellences for yourself, and trying very hard to be (or to appear to be) a servant to others. Viewed from this perspective, obedience seems to be a delusional response to powerlessness. Self-control works out to be denial of most good fleshly things, not the abuse of them. I note that today these "virtues" are not recommended for men, except of course for priests. Today I am looking around, and still do not see the church lauding women for their self-awareness, strength, powerful drive and ebullient sexuality, for example. I want to change humble pie to passion fruit.

As the cult of St. Mary Magdalene grew more popular, however, her symbolic status was heightened. Having the honour of being the first witness of Jesus' resurrection, she is given the title "Apostle of the Apostles." She is the one who comes back from the empty tomb to tell the unbelieving – male – followers the good news. Taking the symbol one step further, she is humanity newly restored to God – the church, the bride of Christ. Apart from the Virgin Mary – and almost equal – she is the supreme female saint. One can see now why the relics of St. Mary Magdalene had to be kept together. The meaning of the saint requires it: penitent, reclaimer of Eve; loving, constant friend; first Christian.

There is one special aspect of the composite Mary Magdalene that is characterized by the basilica of Vézelay itself. It is the one that is dramatized in the gospels of Matthew and Mark by the story of the woman (Mary of Bethany) who comes into the room where Jesus is sitting with his friends and pours precious ointment over his head. When the disciples tut-tut over this lavish expense, saying that the money might have been better spent on the poor, Jesus contradicts them, saying that the woman has anointed him in anticipation of his burial. The hardworking, penny-scraping, literal-minded disciples do not comprehend this idea at all. Paul Tillich devotes one of his sermons to Mary's action, which he calls "holy waste." It is an ecstatic one, he says, going beyond what is reasonable and addressing something of ultimate importance. I think that although Jesus is suggesting that she has foreknowledge of his death, rather than being a religious clairvoyant she is a sort of everyday mystic. She is able to see the significant in the commonplace – here it is a group of comrades having dinner together with an astonishing young preacher, her friend. She is anointing Jesus as the kingly person she knows him to be: for him no gift is too costly. Elisabeth Schüssler Fiorenza says she is the paradigm of the true disciple, in contrast to the uncomprehending disciples who fail to see what the messiahship of Jesus entails. Another intriguing recent find, the second-century *Évangile de Marie*, shows her to be indeed the close friend and interpreter of Jesus' teachings, which are subtle, gnostic in character and way over the heads of the simple fisher folk he is trying to teach. It is as teacher, special friend and mystic that Mary Magdalene should be revered, not as an adulteress who has been straightened out.

Vézelay itself is – it doesn't just stand for – holy waste. By its noble form and worshipful dignity, it reveals something of what ultimacy is. Without these glimpses of the holy, my life would have been impoverished. Surely the countless devoted pilgrims who have passed through here would agree.

For a first-time viewer of the basilica, the capitals of the columns are probably the most intriguing part of the building. There are two lots of capitals, one at more than double my height, the other almost out of sight at the springing of the nave arches, probably about 15 metres up. These extraordinary carvings bring life to the placid strength and self-assurance of the building. In deeply, realistically carved scenes, one for each face of the capital, this "Bible in stone," as one medieval historian calls it, enlightens and frightens the worshippers. I was so fascinated by the skilled work and animation of these vignettes, it took me a while to realize just how bloodthirsty most of them are. Almost all the creatures, human or animal, are acting vigorously; few are standing around chatting, or announcing or revealing. Most have a weapon in their hands, and many of their opponents are taking their last breath. The strange thing is, whether the protagonists are good or evil, violence is their game. David fells Goliath, Moses kills the Egyptian, Absalom is beheaded, Cain receives an arrow in his chest, Ganymede is raped, and two demons fight, as do lions, bears and dragons. Even the angels are the heavy-duty ones: the avenger, and the angel of the last judgment. These warlike gems would have been good propaganda for the recruitment of crusaders.

There are a few peaceable scenes, of meals, of John baptizing Jesus, but even in some of these the tone is brutal. In St. Anthony's vision in the desert he is pulled apart by demons; and in a tame little pastoral scene showing two people eating grapes, one is viciously swallowing a bunch whole, the other grasps his forcefully as if it were a hand grenade.

I am appalled that of all the biblical paradigmatic tales, these were the ones chosen to impress and instruct for all eternity. Many years later I came to realize that "all eternity" was uppermost on everyone's minds, because it was believed to be just around the corner. The sacred hit song of the period could have been, "Prepare yourself, it's later than you think," sung beneath these very clear demonstrations of what would happen if you didn't. I am not alone in my horror that the church could operate on people's feelings that way. Prosper Mérimée, who was responsible for saving Vézelay from becoming a rubble heap, was just as shocked when he first came there in 1835. How could the church have intended to convert people through terror rather than kindness and forgiveness? he wondered.

The mottled, irregularly set stones, the mixture of the damned, the dreary and the virtuous, all seem to complement the mobs of tourists who circulate here, collapse on the steps of the basilica, and meander through the town. They are extremely circumspect inside the church, even those whose interest is probably not religious. The place has that effect upon visitors. Today only one small boy is crying for his lunch. Two sorts of people come here in large crowds: hikers and "grannies." Most of them are day-trippers, walking or busing to the saints. Some have the tough shoes, sweatbands and burdensome backpacks needed for longer journeys, many on their way to Santiago de Compostela, I guess, judging from their lean and bearded looks. Just as in the twelfth century, here are two sorts of pilgrims, some for the neighbouring shrines, some for the long haul, and all going for a multitude of reasons that only the heart itself knows.

It is odd timing, to be writing now about events that happened a thousand years ago. I wonder how the furore and intense expectation that took place so recently compared with what some historians tell us there was after the last turn of the millennium. Mark Kingwell says it did not happen then: around about the year 1000 no calendars agreed as to exact dates, there was no consensus about New Year's Day, and no accurate timekeeping devices. Millennial fever, which struck from time to time, happened later on in the eleventh century. Georges Duby, whose vast knowledge of the Middle Ages runs both broad and deep, says the anticipation of the millennium began in the middle of the tenth century and went on and on. People were concerned about fixing a date, he says, but they didn't know which one it should be: was it 1000 years after Jesus' birth, the year 1000? Or his death, 1033? The actual moment doesn't seem to have been as important as what was going to happen next, because on that particular date, whichever it was, the world was not going to end. It was the date when the "end-time" would begin, which would last for a thousand years until the Last Judgment took place.

This end-time was no joke. In Revelation, St. John spells it out: every kind of disaster that could take place was going to happen. It would be a time of wailing and weeping and misery. It would continue without let-up throughout one's lifetime, and the lifetimes of one's descendants. Then the world would end. Then it was game over for making choices between good and evil.

Millennial anxiety certainly arrived in our time with warnings and doomsaying. What the current prophets seem to be saying, according to Kingwell, is that things are going to be just as bad as they are now, and will probably get worse. It may not be the end, but the end of the world as we know it. How very medieval of them!

Reading Duby's account of the lives of the peasants, I wonder whether they thought the sooner the world ends the better. Imagine all of Europe in the condition of some war-ravaged countries today, and worse. Starvation was the main cause of death, plague the next, followed by murder by thieves or warring groups. No one seemed to die of old age, even those nobles who escaped death in battle. While the plagues tapered off, starvation did not, and monks told stories of people eating other people, even digging up corpses.

Apparently the imminent end-time was cause for terror, because these ghastly occurrences were nothing compared to what was in store. These explicit capitals in the Madeleine with their rousing scenes of violence against the wicked (the good, too, sometimes) must have been enough to cause careful self-scrutiny and confession.

Theologians fanned the flames, some claiming that there were only a limited number of places in heaven; either you had a reservation or you didn't, and there wasn't anything you could do about that. Still, it was best to be good, on the chance that behaviour did count for something. Mainstream theologians said that it was certainly your actions that determined your fate. People in doubt of their rating probably looked up at those explicit, no-nonsense vignettes in fear and trembling.

I would love to find out from a medieval historian what the millenarians said when the apocalypse didn't occur. There is a modern account, *When Prophecy Fails*, by sociologist Lionel Festinger, of the thinking and behaviour of an American millennial group just before and after the date they had expected the world to end. When nothing happened, they rationalized – a date miscalculation – and increased their preparations for their eventual departure from this planet from which they were to be transported by superior beings before it ceased to be. After a second false date, they faded away. More recently, Kingwell describes a group who built underground tunnel shelters in Montana against a nuclear end-time. When the inevitable wasn't, their leader announced that the prayers of the faithful had delayed the event. I wonder if the eleventh-century millenarians handled disappointment and cognitive dissonance in the same way.

What we do know is that life began to improve immeasurably just before the year 1000. Invasions stopped, the political system at home stabilized, and best of all, agriculture got a tremendous boost with the invention of better equipment, and new methods of rotating crops, using land that had been formerly left fallow because it could not be defended. People began to eat regularly. There were still famines and, Duby says, the church often had to lift its ban against eating meat in Lent, because there wasn't any wheat left until the next planting.

In what seems like a strange correlation, architect John James, writing on the architecture of the Middle Ages, says: "Around 1100 people's mortal fear of damnation seems to have been intensifying just as living conditions were improving fast enough to give confidence in the future." He thinks these ambivalent feelings account for the violence of the sculptures at Vézelay. I'd love to know why this unlikely combination of terror about the future and prosperity in the present occurred, if it did. If one looks at the Christian churches in the West over the last few decades, it seems as if they emptied as soon as people's economic situation improved. The only strength, in both faith and numbers, appears in the sectarian groups, who are for the most part at the lower end of the social scale as far as status and earnings are concerned. Today the mainline churches of North America appear to be gaining members in the cities, just as more jobs are in jeopardy and the golden years of instant gratification are over.

The equations: prosperous and confident now = ignore the hereafter, and scraping by/feeling anxious now = court the hereafter, do not seem to apply in the twelfth century. They do not apply to me either, but I'm sure the reasons are quite different. To begin with, I never did have any notion of an angry God who had to be placated, as those medieval people did. That does not mean that I didn't think I had done things that would anger someone; it was that the ones who got angry were right on the spot. As a child they were my parents and myself, and as I got older I took the blame on myself. The God I told about my misbehaviour was completely understanding, although he usually agreed with my assessment. The odd thing is, when things were going badly, I never complained to this God; although I could have used some help, I tried all the mundane, practical options I could think of to improve things. I cannot recall ever asking God to solve my problems on his own. Recently I took a look through a pile of spiritual journals I had kept from university days on, before throwing them out. I noticed that none of the events that made me most miserable at the time were discussed in them – a broken engagement, a job that was eliminated and no other one found for me, a really nasty fight with my father.

On the other hand, whenever there was a time when I felt completely happy, or a moment so joyous I thought I would burst, that is when I told God instantly how grateful I was that he had given me this totally gratuitous pleasure. He was a fair-weather God; in foul weather I didn't bother him. Today, although that image of the deity is long gone, I still catch myself wanting to thank someone for unexpected delights, and send my gratitude out into the biosphere, target unknown.

Vézelay is the church of my religious and Romanesque salad days. When I first came there I had done a lot of wandering in my metaphorical wilderness, a lot of meditating along the sacred way. I had immersed myself in the church's liturgical life; I lived by the church's calendar. I suppose in a sense I had been walking to the saints in circular fashion, revisiting them at the same time every year. Today that phase seems over and antiquated. That cohesive mythic and theologically articulated universe has been punctured, and is collapsing slowly. The old sacred world view still lingers, though, in my wishful, wistful remembrances. One part of me would love to have it back, to be able to be devoted to something splendid and secure, if not someone. The larger part cannot give credence to such a world. Even that discovery at Vézelay of being part of a community of the faithful seems now more sentiment than sense.

Visiting Vézelay that first time was the unconscious start of this pilgrimage. Having seen a Romanesque church of such beauty, I longed to see more. Knowing that the greatest of these were built along the pilgrimage route to Santiago de Compostela, I thought that was the way to approach it: I would make a pilgrimage, ending up in Spain. Along the way I would visit as many churches as I conveniently could. I began to read about pilgrimages, about architecture, about twelfth-century life and thought. I was fascinated.

Many pilgrim sites later, I have come back because my own spiritual pilgrimage requires it. The place has given me something of itself every time I have been here. In this present search I am less a member of a keen, lively community than I was before, not because a community does not exist, but because I cannot fit myself into it with all integrity. I am for the most part alone in the wilderness or on the pilgrim's path, delighted when I meet bright-eyed, honest plodders along the route, hoping for companionship and insight, or – best of miracles – both at once.

Something new is emerging here, though, in this latest visit, a glimpse of the feminine in the divine. For Vézelay is more a woman's place than I realized before. The architecture gives it away. While the tall, narrow nave lifts one up, a strictly ungendered place, the lower, groined ceilings of the aisles are comfortably enclosing. Nurturing in their calm way, they are a shelter, protection under which one travels along the pilgrims' way towards the hidden feminine relic. The basilica is not the bastion of the crusaders. It is not warlike, though it is thrilling, and its sculpture stimulates thoughts of violence. The contrast is startling, between the triumphalist crusaders' aims and the symbol of the saint – her intimacy with Jesus, her intuitive, symbolic honouring of him, even when it seemed that he and his cause were dead. Then there is the incongruity of the vicious, threatening sculptures set in an utterly beautiful, all-encompassing milieu, the basilica as the model of heaven on earth. I read that medieval people were accustomed to holding contradictory thoughts and sentiments at the same time. We really are not so different. There are few seamless events, moods or feelings in my life; the best of them are always spotted by mean thoughts, or inappropriate occurrences. I can hardly think of an occasion where everything about it was simply complete, or where I didn't get anxious or distracted or blow my stack about something. Even in church? Yes, especially in church!

Walking in the early morning in the park surrounding the east end of the basilica, trying to register and absorb all the curving lines of its gracious form, I can see that the whole hilltop is isolated from the rest of the countryside. From the brow of the hill the apse is visible through a shimmer of wet chestnut trees, and below and beyond it the wide valley is curtained off by a thin white mist. Mist. Mystic. Mystery. Yes.

CHAPTER 3

— TOURS —

Martin. *Saint. b.* 317, *Pannonia; d.* 397, *Candes, France. Soldier in imperial Roman army. After giving half his cloak to a naked beggar, received a visitation from Christ who said, "You have clothed me." Baptized, monk at 45, bishop at 55. Performed many miracles of healing and resuscitation without fanfare. Held winning arguments with the devil in human disguise. Known widely as a peacemaker, founder of churches, destroyer of idols, moral spokesman to emperors.*

Lorraine, Joan of. *Saint. b.* 1412, *Domrémy; d.* 1431, *Rouen. Directed by the voices of saints Catherine, Margaret and Michael to rid France of the English. Defeated them at Beaugency and Orléans. Captured at Compiègne. Sold by the Duke of Luxembourg to the English for* 10,000 *francs. Tried for heresy, condemned and burned. Rehabilitated, sentence annulled,* 1456. *Canonized,* 1920.

If I had known beforehand what I would find in Tours I surely would never have gone there. This is the town to which I had prematurely awarded three stars in my roster of medieval riches. Since it was the gathering point for the most frequented route to Santiago de Compostela, it was bound to be a fine blend of sacred lore and noble architecture. Besides that, Martin, its patron saint, was the one most highly venerated in the Middle Ages, on a par with the apostles. The city's very name, meaning towers, is enough to stimulate my imagination: in my mind's eye I saw delicate turrets, thin spires, crenellated battlements, Renaissance palaces – a skyline that assembles all the ages into one dazzling picture. All this and the placid Loire too.

I don't remember much about our previous visit to Tours, when Bob and I stopped there briefly on our first trip to France in 1966. I guess I wasn't thinking about the presence or absence of towers then. We stayed in a drab little hotel not far from the cathedral, and spent most of our time trying to capture on film the wondrous colours of the stained-glass windows there, the first Renaissance glass we had ever seen. Unused to the particular ambience of French towns, we thought its down-at-heel look made it seem interesting.

Years later, it is a little less down-at-heel but what is interesting has been whittled down to a sliver. I wouldn't mind so much, except for knowing that during the Middle Ages it was the most frequented shrine and place of pilgrimage in Europe, a city of learning, full of treasures and miraculous happenings. During the Renaissance it flourished on silk; its inhabitants reportedly dressed magnificently and drank from gold cups. Then I discover Henry James writing about this home of Balzac with the keenness of eye and delight that only he can command, finding charming and curious urban parallels between the settings of the older man's novels and what he sees in front of him. James writes about the eighteenth-century buildings on the rue Royale, for instance; since he was there in 1882 the rue Royale has become rue Nationale. All the handsome buildings were destroyed in World War II.

I think if you were to start out for Santiago de Compostela from here today, your enthusiasm would be dimmed on the first night. Tours is the quintessential nonentity. It has all your basic tourism needs – two rivers, two cathedrals, one château, several museums, some good food, an old centre – but no special tone. Even the river bears no curious traffic, which is perhaps why the strip of parkland beside it is empty except for one running boy and his dog. The vast city hall square, a typical nineteenth-century design, has been abandoned by ceremony, leaving only faded pomp in charge. I feel right at home, as though I have been here many times. The shops, the brasseries, the street names, all are like those in any mid-size French city.

Among the ordinary sounds of an ordinary town, the only fully directed energy comes from the beggars. There are lots of them, with plenty to say, some confrontational. A dark and toothless woman, everyone's bogeygypsy, doesn't curse me, but almost. Another man, when refused, says smilingly that he would like to do something very nasty to my mother. I am glad to get away from this violence, remembering that Freud told us there are no jokes. Is this the worst of paradoxes, that in St. Martin's town, whose famed act of generosity was to share his cloak with a beggar, today's beggars are so dastardly in the way they look and importune you that I am unwilling to share anything, not even a word?

There are still masses of pilgrims coming here, all taking day trips to visit the châteaux of the Loire, for which the city is a handy base.

Two people I spoke to warmed up immediately when I said I was here to visit Tours, not the châteaux. Tourists go from here in guided flocks, just like their pilgrim predecessors. Unlike the latter, though, they are not here to honour St. Martin.

Ever since Martin's day people have walked to the saints with special desires in mind. Sometimes it was for the holy purpose of venerating the saints' relics or going to the places where the saints had been. At other times it was in search of a cure. Gradually a kind of medico-theological specialization took place. Not every saint could help every illness; often people had to search out the appropriate saint, going from shrine to shrine. St. Eutrope was good for dropsy, for instance; those with that malady would head for Saintes. St. Roch and St. Étienne warded off the plague. One determined pilgrim who suffered from migraines went to every shrine in Burgundy. Finally he was cured after praying to St. Benoît for three weeks at a certain priory. St. Martin was much more versatile, *premier grand cru* one might say. Martin's fifth-century biographer says that he raised three people from the dead, and healed many others during his lifetime. Further down the pilgrim road, in the cloister at Moissac, there is a scene on one of the capitals showing Martin bringing back to life a new convert who died before being baptized, a severe crisis requiring his help. Martin's cures are always performed quietly and on the basis of serious need. There is no showmanship about him. After his death, people could be cured simply by touching his tomb.

The standard guidebook for pilgrims in the twelfth century, part of the *Liber Sancti Jacobi*, says that only four saints' bodies still remain intact in their coffins, of which St. Martin's is one. No wonder the pilgrim hordes continued to come here. I wonder if there is any relationship between the efficacy of the saint and the establishment of the Valois court in palaces nearby. Through a kind of contiguous magic, something like the royal touch in reverse, kings may have hoped to live long and healthily in the saint's orbit.

So here I am, in the wake of all these people, kings and pilgrims, walking to the saint in this town, looking for – not a cure exactly, but something to warm the cockles, stir the spirit, or even whet the visual appetite. So far, nothing has done so. I go off to find the basilica with Martin's tomb.

I did not expect to find the original one, built in the fifth century. The Normans razed it. Another vast basilica was constructed in the eleventh century, in order to house the hordes of pilgrims. The Huguenots were the destroyers this time, and it was never rebuilt. Today all that is left are two of its massive square towers, dourly attached to a drab commercial street. They are spaced so widely apart, with several houses now between them, that you can fill in the gap and imagine the size of the basilica. It was, according to eyewitnesses, the same shape as the cathedral at Santiago de Compostela, though not quite as vast. It must have dominated the townscape. Today the towers are a truly mournful sight, the one, the so-called Clock Tower, nudged by an unbecoming set of buildings, the other, the Tour de Charlemagne, a patched-up skeleton standing alone in an unkempt enclosure, almost a warning to those who build too big and too grand. It is surely ironic that in a city called Towers, these are almost the only sorry remains.

After trailing along the empty high and low streets on a Sunday afternoon, I eventually come to the Old Town Square, place Plumereau, which turns out to be a pleasant half-timbered affair, narrow houses with steep pointed roofs like newspapers on your head to keep off the rain. It has been made into a giant outdoor café and boutiquerie, all tourists' wares at tourists' prices, nothing I haven't run into a hundred times before. Looking down the side streets I can see great vistas of plastic chairs indicating food dished out on the street, in what are euphemistically called cafés. Places to drop your shopping bags and body after examining St. Martin's bones in the nearby basilica. St. Bernard understood and criticized this mind-set in his day: of the faithful who came to see the vainglorious churches, he said, "Their eyes feast on the relics and the strings of their purses are undone."

Poor St. Martin. His head and his arm are still in town – in the replacement nineteenth-century basilica which I peeked inside and quickly left – but his soul must certainly have moved on. Not entirely, perhaps: the people of Tours are still proud that the armistice of World War I was signed on St. Martin's Day, November 11. An appropriate choice, I suppose, for a city that was devastated by wartime attacks. Martin's only fitting memorials today are those superb windows in the cathedral of St. Gatien, a local luminary who brought Christianity to this part of France in the third century. With the exception of a few added stains and repairs, these brilliantly told episodes in the life of St. Martin must have looked just the same to the thirteenth-century pilgrims who first saw them. The cathedral, however, is not an endearing place to me; these windows are the only jewels in its crown.

This is a city whose fragments give rise to pathos, and to thoughts of what might have been. What were all those towers that gave the city its name? How did they fall? We know about the horrendously frequent external militancy that broke up its fabric; we don't know if there was also an internal corrosion, a self-destruct perhaps, that brought it down to this humdrum level. Could it ever have been the true city of St. Martin? Impossible.

The story of the life of St. Martin is that of an ascetic, holy Christian, who is generous, thoughtful, never a seeker for glory, to the extent that crowds of people had to come and drag him from his monastery to force him to become their bishop. No one today would accept the stories of his accomplishments, or the qualities ascribed to him, as historically accurate. Biographies (or *Vitae*) in the early Christian era followed a set formula, based on the Greek literary model for the praising of heroes, called the *bios*. According to the reasoning behind the *bios*, because Martin was a great saint, he would have had to perform certain actions: discussions with the devil and the emperor, restoration of the dead. There was no doubt about their truth. Besides, in this case Martin's biographer was one of his most devoted disciples, a former Roman senator.

Even so, Martin comes through his *Vita* today as special. The main thing you realize is how much he resembles Jesus. He dresses humbly, gives away everything and so owns nothing, and is devoted in prayer. When he is going to heal someone, he asks everyone to leave the room, and never talks about his success. (Jesus used to ask the cured person not to tell anyone about it.) Martin drives out devils, forgives heretics. On a couple of occasions women have come in to bathe his feet with oil: one of them was the empress. Clearly they could see the resemblance.

No city and probably few of its citizens could come anywhere close to imitating the actions and motivations of this saint. Still, there were some qualities of Martin's way of life that were held up to ordinary people to emulate. They were encouraged to acts of kindness and generosity towards each other, and particularly towards strangers. To make the point clear, there were incredible stories about the best and worst that could happen if you didn't behave charitably. In nearby Poitiers there is the tale of the two pilgrims returning from Santiago de Compostela without a sou and who knocked on all doors in one quarter of the town, asking for bed and board. Everyone turned them down except for the last person they tried. Soon afterwards, a fire burned down the entire quarter with the exception of this charitable man's house. People were expected to shelter pilgrims, with what promises of rewards I do not know, yet there are many horror tales about men accosting pilgrims near the Spanish border, demanding protection money. On the saintly side, there is the unbeatable example of Hugues, abbot of Cluny. Two knights arrived at the monastery seeking sanctuary. The reason: they had killed Hugues' father and brother, and were being pursued for the murders. When the monk who opened the door to them came to tell Hugues, he ordered him to let them in.

Charity seems to have been a virtue of the professional religious, but I wonder how far it extended into the lives of the knights, or the peasants. It is hard to know how the peasants acted towards one another, as they couldn't write and no one was interested in writing about them. Emmanuel Le Roy Ladurie's account of the people of Montaillou in the fourteenth century shows them to be sociable, help- ful to each other, but only within certain particular groupings, those of women and clans. Women came together for mutual support to build up their armoury against men – information – and did each other favours as a matter of course. Their communal sense extended beyond status lines, and a gentlewoman's closest friends might be peasants, if there were no other nobility around. Clans stayed together to main- tain social control, and at this particularly dangerous time, to avoid being condemned for heresy by the Inquisition. As for the nobility, judging from the sort of brutality with which members of the great families treated each other, I suspect charity was employed either publicly to gain some ulterior reward, or not at all. They were inter- ested in this world, all right, but as Lord Thomson of Fleet once said, "Kindness doesn't sell papers." Nor does it maintain feudal estates, breed heirs, keep brothers off your land.

Motivations do not change much. My notion of charity is partial, circumscribed and a lot more self-interested than I would like to believe. I begin to see another reason why Tours gives me the blues, and it is not the city's fault: I wonder, what on earth have I to do with Martin, first-class saint?

If there is any similarity, it is a superficial one, and has nothing to do with saintliness. I notice that Martin's life is always a combination of opposites, and always changing. First he is an army officer and kind to peasants, which is atypical for a soldier. Then he becomes a Christian and so a conscientious objector, yet stays in the army: he becomes a soldier of Christ, as he puts it. The soldier becomes a monk, and the monk becomes a bishop, and yet remains a monk. So he wears camels' skins, retreats to a cave with his brethren to pray, and at the same time travels through his diocese administering justice and theology. There is no one like him, and yet his mission is clear and simple: to extend and deepen people's faith at home and afar.

A friend of mine pointed out to me recently that I am always "re-inventing" myself. That sounded pretty funny, but when I thought about it I realized it was part of a bigger program, which is about being different. I can't remember a time when I didn't want to be different from what I thought was the run-of-the-mill. Not very different, just somewhat. I think it must have come from a realization when I was in my teens that I would never do anything perfectly satisfactorily. Whether in any competition with others, or measured against my own standard, I would never be numero uno. It was very important that this should not be known. So, to close the gap, to see myself as more than pretty capable, I would not follow the straight track, but choose another way, one that twisted this way and that, confusing the enemy, my needy self. Hence the reinvention of myself.

The plan – for at the beginning it was a conscious intention – shows its outlines in every aspect of my life: career, friendships, religion, houses. I suppose there have been some threads running through it in a more or less connected way, though it does seem on the surface like the charmed life of a self-centred humanist, pottering about and getting nowhere. It hasn't been. The yearning for a developing spiritual life has run through it, sometimes with great passion, sometimes shallowly. For a time the light was turned off, but I was not too discouraged, knowing that growth takes place in the dark too. It has been years since I ever had the clarity of vision that resembles Martin's, and never was I propelled to such single-minded action as his. While he seems to have made a beeline for the ultimate, my life is more like the motion of the bees beside our "Colomba's" wall, circling in and out around the jasmine, never staying still for long.

There is another characteristic Martin and I share. One of his biographers comments that he is always moving about, never at home in any place for long. This is because, says the writer quoting Hebrews, he seeks another country, which is the heavenly one.

I love houses, of many different types. At one time I thought I would be able to live in every type I admired, over the course of my life. We have lived in eight houses over forty years of marriage. Most of the moves have been necessitated by job changes, but all of the houses have been chosen out of some vision of what will bring together home and personality, or self-image. I have a suspicion that these moves are in part dictated by changes in self-recognition, or unrealized desire, though I have not always been aware of it. We have never bought a house because it was efficient, practical or complete.

The underlying movement that leads to changes in houses, in new attempts to create the just-right home, are somehow linked to these walks to the saints that I keep undertaking year after year, though I don't know exactly how. The best I can do at this point is to say that both are searches from the heart to find a place where the heart is at home. I don't need to remind myself of St. Augustine's "the heart is restless till it rest in Thee," but I cannot make that connection yet. I know that "Colomba" represents an important aspect of that home the heart seeks; visits to the saints are like forays to collect the pieces of furniture – the soul stuff, and whatever else I find – to put the whole house together. My search for home is nothing like Martin's, though: his restlessness comes from the fervour of wanting to bring the whole world to God. To do this, you cannot sit still.

One of the most renowned of homeless people was Joan of Arc, who was physically uprooted and yet spiritually centred. She is memorialized everywhere in this part of France, where she accomplished her great work. I found my first reference to her, just as I was deciding to give up on Tours altogether, in the small Musée de Campagnonnage, situated on the rue Nationale in part of an old cloister that did not get bombed. The *compagnons* were members of an association of highly skilled craftsmen, who have made everything from carriages to pâtis-serie. The association, medieval in origin, continues to this day. Here I discover that some local *compagnons* had made Joan's armour and stan-dard. She stayed in Tours, in another tower I missed, on her way to raise the siege of Orléans, and came back again after her victory to be thanked by the soon-to-be-crowned Charles VII. Then, after all that glory, when she was captured everyone let her down. Today there is hardly a sizeable French town without a statue of Joan in armour, sometimes, as in Toulouse, on horseback.

There were many reasons for her trial and execution and hurried rehabilitation. She had rallied the French to a nationalism they were too weak and dispirited to achieve on their own. To the English Joan was worth a big heap of poker chips in this interminable game of war; the French "ally" was willing to sell. The trial seems to have been a political set-up and at the same time a nightmare of anti-feminism. It seemed witchcraft was on the increase; for every sorcerer these days, said the grand inquisitor, there were 10,000 witches. It was therefore clear to those French clerics who sided with the English that, given those odds, Joan's voices were devilish and she was a witch.

Besides this cogent logic, I wonder if Joan was found guilty because she took a man's role, fought like a man? One of the main accusations against her was that she dressed in armour and men's cloth-ing, which was "an abomination before God." If those inquisitors could be here today! I don't suppose it occurred to them that they dressed more like women in their liturgical splendour. Cross-dressing is a political matter too.

The unofficial explanation of her rehabilitation was that Charles VII, who did nothing to save Joan, did not want it thought that he owed his crown to a heretic. The more significant meaning of her life, trial and death, which the rehabilitators ignored – that she held out for the truth of her individual experience against what the powers-that-be told her was the truth – is what makes her so very contemporary, and so much a saint. She is ahead of her time, an advance guard linked both to Protestantism and to the ideals of the French Revolution. To say I know, when everyone else believes otherwise, must be an incredibly brave and lonely thing to do. Imagining her, trapped by all those vindictive or blinkered people, yet still holding on to what she truly knows, makes me grieve over her anguish and the wickedness of the world that caused it.

I cannot think when I have ever taken a leap out of the known, acceptable world of opinions on the strength of my own exclusive experience. Today, for instance, when I am so upset at the lassitude of the church with respect to sexism and bad theology, I could, if I dared, leave all that behind and take my own solitary stand in the world. It would be a Christian stand all the same. Yet I am afraid to lose the baby with the bathwater, which is probably an excuse, an explanation for why Joan is who she is and I am a wavering coward.

Joan is one of those rare people who have been taken for the devil's handmaid one day, and a near-saint the next. She was actually not canonized until 1920. It is weird, but it figures. For the English, Joan was a terrible threat: her visions were affecting the war with grave results for them; therefore she must be a witch. For the French, after the politics of war were over, the victories to which her visions led made her a saint. For the church, she was dangerous, the way she slipped out from under its authority, letting the voices of her saints take precedence over accepted behaviour. Her beliefs, however, were always indisputably orthodox; it was just that darn suit of clothes!

The great thing about Joan's story is that she is not an archetype but someone whose authentic voice can be heard through the records of her trial. She's one glowing answer to the belief that all women are Eve and therefore the cause of the world's downfall. But just as surely as the traditional image of the penitent Mary Magdalene is no role model for women today, neither is Joan. She's a kind of warrior nun, totally focussed on her goal, without thought of *Kinder* and *Küche* or other earthly delights. Twenty years ago that was the *optimum bonum* for militant feminists; today the feminist image has been enlarged, or modified – take your pick – to be more inclusive or watered-down. Joan is just as impossible to imitate as Martin. Still, here in the region that was the small kingdom of France in her day, she is heroic, a bright light in this dim and discouraging town.

Jacques Paul, writing about the church and its relationship to culture, says that the cult of saints had three foci, sometimes joined together, more often not. Saints were used for their miraculous powers, for liturgical celebrations, and as models for living. Joan does not seem to have been particularly noted for the miracles ascribed to her. There is no special liturgical celebration for her, nor are there today many churches in her name, though there may have been in the past. As a model for living, she is out. She is, if you can call it that, more a secular saint, or a national hero, to all those who love her, but do not worship at her shrines. Le Roy Ladurie says she combines all the functions of the three orders – peasant, warrior, religious – as they were set out in the early Middle Ages, and that this gave her such broad acclaim. But in our day, it is almost as if the church, having canonized her, did not quite know what to do with her.

These two saints, a thousand years apart, have strikingly affected the fortunes of France. Both Joan and Martin were launched on their spiritual quests, driven, you might say, by heavenly messages they could not ignore. They made no mistake about where credit was due; one was revered for it, the other condemned. A cynic would say it's all in the timing.

I return to the two forlorn towers, saddened by the failed vision that is this church and this city, which once held the likes of Martin and Joan. An analogy comes to mind as I think about the biblical description of the New Jerusalem, the holy city that was to appear at the end of the millennium, and how the twelfth-century scholars turned the idea on its head. Before this time, says Colin Morris, people believed that the city would come down from heaven, bringing the eternal into the temporal and changing it essentially and forever. The kingdom would exist on a "new earth," as Revelation says. This would be the city Martin set about to build. In the twelfth century this belief changed: a gloomier mood and different attitude to living caused the writers to look heavenward to situate the New Jerusalem. They said that the individual must wait here on earth sorrowfully, longing to reach her true home, the Jerusalem which is beyond this world, in the hereafter. This is a major relocation with all sorts of consequences, and one that has affected popular belief ever since. To me, those towers, separated from each other today by small-time commerce and dirty sidewalks, are victims of the disappearance of the old vision. Once they were part of a divine program that heralded a Jerusalem to come, that would turn the very streets of Tours into a smooth, golden path for all the saints to walk upon.

Today I am inclined towards that earlier view, even if it seems impossibly optimistic. Although there's no going back in time and thought exactly, I think whatever dream I have of the New Jerusalem comes a lot closer to the pre-medieval one. To trust in a glorious here-after where everything we botched up here will be fixed, smoothed out and given a coat of gold and polychrome, seems like a cop-out that is unworthy of us. This is the world we have been given, even if I don't know why, in which we try to do our loving best to reclaim it for everyone. Tours today is a metaphorical picture of how far we still have to go. The image of the radiant city coming down and settling on the earth is a wonderful way for me to picture the hoped-for transformation.

With its broken towers and fallen aspirations, Tours has had a deflat-ing effect on me, enough for me to ask myself if I am really a pilgrim. Why am I doing this? What do I expect to gain? Maybe I just can't sit still for long and that's all there is to it. No high spiritual purpose, just itchy feet, a curious eye, and a mind that finds itself empty of history and wants to collect some old fragments to shore up my ruins. Dissatisfaction with the present time appearing under the false colours of a sophisticated aim: a pilgrimage. Is this reductionism or realism?

I shall blame my doubts on the city, and change my expectations for it. Tours is not a high holy place. What should have been glistening towers and prayer-scented sanctuaries for my expectant eyes is a mélange of tedious blocks of faceless buildings, a jumble of ruins and a waning nostalgia.

No, I should blame my disappointment on myself, knowing that Tours is a sort of threshold for me over which I am afraid to pass. Its dullness is an emotional intervention: I know the feeling well. There have been many thresholds where I have stood dumbly, vacillating between fear of the consequences and the allure of what's new. Sometimes I have propelled myself over, even though some intuition warned me not to, and the results have been miserable. Then there have been other clearly marked thresholds which, when I chose to step gingerly over them, led to the best things in my life: marriage, children, teaching. Once, almost forty years ago, from an unexamined position as a dutiful Christian, I stood on the threshold of a compelling faith and discovered that on the other side was a no-fooling path of utter seriousness. It was a terrible experience, during which I waffled, I rationalized, I rode a roller coaster of doubt and fear that blocked out everything else I was doing. Eventually I propelled myself over. I can recall the almost throttling terror of it, of asking, "My God, what have I done?" and knowing that the answer was, "Too late! You can't go back now."

Setting out to visit the saints with a lot of doubts and anger in my pack, along with the eagerness and delight, has not had the same wrenching beginning. There is more of a lurking uneasiness, a sneaking notion that perhaps I will be affected with the same sort of blow from Maxwell's silver hammer that occurred to me before. Only this time I am mature, I can handle it, I tell myself. Then I know I am just kidding myself as usual, and am probably asking for more than I know or have bargained for.

Whatever my motives, mixed as they are, I am apparently no different from those medieval strugglers. Lots of people went on pilgrimage for most unholy reasons. Besides those who were going out of real devotion, there were many who were sent there as penance for their sins/crimes. The worst of these were condemned to travel in chains until these rusted and fell off. Some had to go barefoot. Probably most ended up barefoot, the going was so rough.

There were other types of pilgrims whose reasons, good or bad, had nothing to do with holiness, indulgences or absolution. There were the heretics. These were probably Cathars, thinks Yves Dossat, writing on the weird varieties of pilgrims. Cathars were members of a popular puritanical movement, with heretical beliefs about the nature of the universe, and a determinedly ascetic way of life. Dossat doesn't say why they were travelling. Was it to make converts, or to flee the Inquisition? Then there were persons travelling in disguise, to avoid other warring groups. One soldier took off in order to postpone paying his debts to his captain. Women who wanted to get away from their husbands could use a pilgrimage as a legitimate escape. There were the real phonies, called *coquillards*, out to fleece the lambs. Some people went for the "foolish pleasure" of it. Finally, there were professional pilgrims, on hire by others who could not make the trip themselves. Some people made a living this way. I can't help speculating about the lifestyle of one countess, who over the space of sixteen years sent eight pilgrims to Santiago de Compostela in her name. Eventually the church authorities became disturbed at the number of false penitents who might endanger the way for the genuine ones, and decided to put a cap on pilgrimage: penitents would do penance at home.

It must have been hell on family life. There is a tale about a professional pilgrim whose wife partied the money away while he was gone. When he returned he was furious and struck her so hard that she died soon after, whereupon he fled the country. He was exonerated from the crime, however, with the help of his friends, who argued that his wife's conduct brought on the reprisal. Just another one of those little inequities of the social system. Things must have improved in the next hundred years or so, otherwise why would another pilgrim, the lusty, genial – and rich – Wife of Bath, be off on the road looking for husband number six?

I guess the clergy are today's professional pilgrims, providing the religious framework and the services that people still think are essential to have but not to perform themselves. Imagine a professional pilgrim's business card: "Will walk, pray, suffer for you. All popular shrines visited. All relics venerated. Martyrs a specialty. Circle tour or one way. Reasonable rates." Then imagine a priest's or minister's today: "Will pray daily. All rites of passage in suitable surroundings. We also do Sundays. Very reasonable rates."

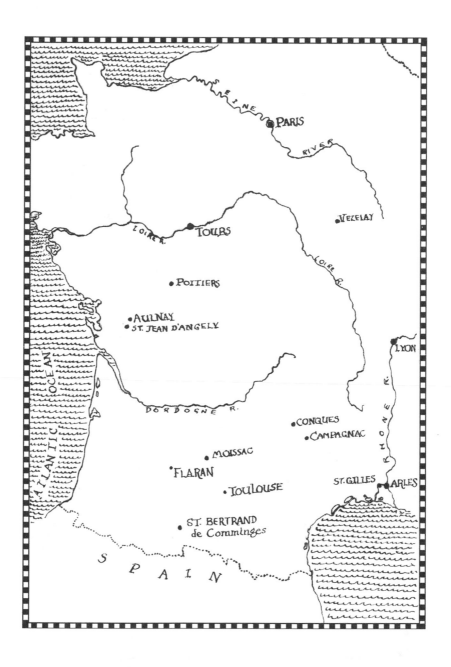

Notre Dame le grande · Poitiers   en plicant 1921

CHAPTER 4

— POITIERS —

Mary, Virgin. *Saint. b? 1st century B.C., Palestine; d? 1st century A.D., Palestine. Wife of Joseph of Nazareth. Mother of Jesus by the Holy Spirit, as declared by the angel Gabriel. Postbiblical theology says that at her death she was taken directly to heaven to reign beside Jesus. Intercedes with him on behalf of humanity. Among her titles: Our Lady, Queen of Heaven, Mother of God.*

Hilaire, or Hilarius. *Saint. b. 315, Poitiers; d. 368, Poitiers. Son of Roman senator. Probable first bishop of Poitiers. Noted teacher, whose most famous pupil was Martin of Tours. After his death miracles took place at his tomb.*

Radegonde. *Saint. b. circa 520, Thuringia; d. 587, Poitiers. Princess of Thuringia, Queen of the Franks. Later a nun, who founded the convent of Sainte-Croix, where she died. Patron saint of Poitiers.*

Aquitaine, Eleanor of. *Duchess, Countess of Poitiers, Queen of France, Queen of England. b. 1124, Bordeaux or Belin; d. 1204, Fontevraud. Married at 13 to Dauphin, later Louis VII. Marriage annulled March 21, 1152. Married duc d'Anjou, later Henry II of England, May 18, 1152, at Poitiers. Between ages of 29 and 34 had five children. Imprisoned by Henry 1173-1189. Ruled Aquitaine and England through her sons from 1189 until her death.*

Mélusine. *Goddess/fairy. Origin Celtic (?). Daughter of a king and a fairy. Married Raimondin, lived in Lusignan near Poitiers with their ten sons. Departed suddenly when her husband broke his marital oath. Said to visit her old château to warn of disasters and deaths.*

T he only thing I knew about Poitiers before I went there was that there was one great pilgrimage church still standing that maintains its eleventh-century characteristics. So many Romanesque buildings along the pilgrimage routes have been destroyed, left in fragments or given unbecoming facelifts that, like the relics of saints, it is hard to find a whole one in more or less good condition.

The basilica of Saint-Hilaire, although rebuilt often, seemed to meet my criteria. This was the object of my first visit. I knew nothing of the rest of the city, chock-a-block with sacred sites, one built as early as the fourth century. Above all, I had not reckoned on the women, for Poitiers is a city that has welcomed, remembered and honoured women: holy, worldly, legendary. In my starry-eyed view, it does so still. Day after day I found myself, with a doggedness that conquered my exhaustion, walking to the saints and women's places again and again.

What a contrast Poitiers is to Tours! Here is a real city, aging and ageless, a patchwork and a palimpsest that works. Unlike Tours, there is no cleanly "restored" old quarter. The city seems to have absorbed its history unself-consciously. Of course its inhabitants have made mistakes, tearing down the wrong things and building nonentities. That's normal: no family growing up keeps all of its mementos or treasures. Poitiers has done pretty well by them, though.

The city has been lucky, from the point of view of patrimony if nothing else. It never attracted big powers, whether secular or ecclesiastical, so it didn't have to undergo the destruction of major symbolic buildings by new regimes eager to make their own statement. It was Eleanor of Aquitaine's city, part of her inheritance from her father, and although she didn't live here for very long, her contribution was cultural rather than warlike. It did have one brief, glorious period in the sixteenth century, when it was the seat of the very cultured Jean, duc de Berry. Because Poitiers was not bombed during World War II, there were no gaps to fill in with misconceived contemporary architectural abominations. Most of what passes for twentieth-century architecture here has been kept outside the city proper, this little isthmus in the middle of two rivers, the Boivre and the Clain, a tributary of the Loire.

Years ago the name Poitiers was engraved in my memory by Lewis Mumford, who claimed that the direction of the tide of history was changed here thanks to one marvellous Gallic invention: the stirrup. With horses so equipped, Charles Martel (The Hammer), Charlemagne's grandfather, was able to defeat the Arab armies and send them packing, thus saving Gaul for the French. I never heard anything more about the city beyond that date, AD 732, until I started investigating the pilgrimage routes.

Even before I discovered the many religious foundations that embellish the city, I was captivated by Poitiers' everyday face. It is fully alive, flesh and soul, home to bikers with yellow rooster-combed hair, couples with sun-shaded strollers, students eating slices of pizza on the go, crowds of citizens filling the cafés in the squares and streets leading off them. It is hard to spot a tourist here; maybe they are all French, but from away; otherwise how can so many people spend so much time drinking coffee or beer or pastis?

Here is the neo-Renaissance Hôtel de Ville with its great square, surrounded on three sides by umbrella-shaded tables. In the open space parents watch their very young practising daredevil manoeuvres on their gaudy bicycles braced with training wheels. A two-year-old wearing a lime-green helmet is playing soccer with his dad. Another boy is teetering around on blue and orange roller skates. Today this square is the hub of the city, mainly, I suppose, because of its frame-work: the large Printemps department store facing the Hôtel de Ville, and the once-elegant theatre, now a cinema, on the third side.

Walking the steep streets I try to imagine what the town was like 900 years ago. It must have been large, as the main religious edifices are so far apart. Like Montréal, it probably spread to its natural bound-aries, the rivers, and then stopped for a long time until defence was no longer a problem. On this triangular isthmus, where was the centre, I wondered? The earliest extant building, the fourth-century baptistery, is close to the river, but that would surely not have been the centre of the medieval town.

The religious centre of the city today is probably the twelfth-century Nôtre-Dame-la-Grande, standing serenely beautiful in a broad, brick and stone paved square soaking up admiration from the crowds in the adjacent cafés or shopping at the market stalls that surround it. In keeping with its unpretentious character, there is no one great approach to it; instead a number of modest streets curve into the square here and there. So there is no build up, nothing to prepare you for the incredible façade, a panoply of stone carving. It appears in many books on Romanesque architecture, but nothing touches the real thing. The overall design is not unique: other churches have used the same formal outlines. It is the work itself that is so ambitious and so stirringly executed.

There are five physical stages to the sculptural program. The central door with its four rounded, carved architraves, is flanked by two similarly designed blind arcades, each containing a supporting twinned column arcade. Above these, a frieze topped by a cornice runs across the façade. Stages three and four are two rows of arcades, fourteen in all, in which sit or stand the twelve apostles and two notables, probably St. Hilaire and St. Martin. Another cornice, and then above it all is the great pediment, with Christ standing before his cross, not on it, within the ancient oval form of the mandorla. His guardians at each end of the pediment are two turrets with stone roofs like pinecones, resting on a triad of columns. These form the outer rim of the façade, and hold it together visually, keeping it grounded.

Battered and weather-beaten though it is, the figures facing more and more decrepitude while they await their turn to be restored, the façade conveys a lively, theological/biblical narrative. The faces, human and animal, that fill in the décor have a weird contemporary look about them.

The story told in vignettes on the frieze over the central door is mainly Mary's story: the Annunciation, the Visitation to Elizabeth to tell her of her pregnancy, and the Birth of Jesus. Joseph appears once, in his usual position on the sidelines with his hand supporting his head. The figure of Jesse is inserted just after the Annunciation, followed by Jesse's famous son, King David.

This reminds me of a little lineage problem that no one has tackled satisfactorily. Matthew's gospel traces Jesus' lineage all the way from Adam, through David to the family in Nazareth. The only problem with this (well, certainly not the only one) is that the line is traced down to Joseph, and we know just how much he had to do with Jesus' birth. The David connection, giving Jesus a fine royal ancestry, is a well-meaning device.

We don't know anything about Mary's line, except for her mother's name, Anne, and her father's, Joachim. A rather misogynistic friend of mind used laughingly to quote the lines "Good Saint Anne, send me a man as fast as you can." I suppose that is what people thought Mary wanted, along with every other woman. Once he turned up, the woman would be taken into her husband's household to further the husband's line. In Jesus' case, however, there was no male lineage; Mary was the only human parent.

The twelfth-century thinkers decided to cope with this in their own peculiar way. Duby says that at this time people were very concerned about having lengthy noble ancestry, and began constructing family trees. At the same time theologians wanted to reinforce the idea that Jesus was truly human as well as truly divine – a tough one, I grant them – in a battle they were having with other thinkers who said he wasn't really human, just an appearance of God. So they gave Jesus a family tree too. The most famous illustration of this is the Tree of Jesse window in Chartres cathedral showing Jesus' lineage from King David to Mary (not Joseph) to himself. On the human side, his ancestry was both royal and pertinent.

Although Mary inherited noble status, socially she didn't have a chance. It would take more than even the belief in Jesus' singular birth to undermine a patrilineal society. Biblical peoples had a lot of trouble with powerful women: Jezebel, Salome, Eve, and others they called witches. Order and control of society through the woman's line would be unthinkable.

So the early theologians, not perceiving, or preferring to ignore the fact, that the lineage account came from one Evangelist and the Virgin Birth account from another, decided to hold two impossible thoughts at once, as they are wont to do, and leave David as Jesus' ancestor. *Nihil disturbat.*

With a weird capacity for contradictions in thought and feeling that the Romanesque sculptors seem to have been addicted to, the façade has its ferocious, unholy side. The capitals and the blind arcades along the front are entirely inhabited by monsters, grotesque animals, or wild creatures doing their utmost to swallow or disgorge others. There is a young woman, her hands folded prayerfully, being eaten by two lions; beside her another naked human shields himself from the jaws of a gigantic pair of beasts. Another pair is engorging or disgorging a frog-shaped creature, and another pair has just devoured everything but a whiskered head. All the other animals in this savage panoply are fighting or, if they are alone, biting themselves. There is an entire frieze of these self-mutilators. Was it the year of the plague of fleas? Wherever you look on this bottom rank of the façade you can see that the low life there is really low life. There seems to be no connection between these motifs and the story of the coming of Jesus, just above their heads.

This odd assemblage suggests to me that the medieval world view was either much more complex than I realize, or more compartmentalized. I expect stories, whether in print or in stone, to make sense, to be whole, just as I expect them to get the family tree right. I think my problem here is that I want this sculptured story to give up its meaning as simply as if it were a cartoon. I expect instant recognition: I know who and what all the figures are so why shouldn't the meaning of the whole be easily grasped? This is quite absurd, since I would never demand such simplistic revelation from a verbal narrative, whether folk tale, myth or literature. In each case there are rules to be learned, background to be studied, context understood, before the meaning of the story becomes clear. It is never self-evident after a glance. If it were, teachers of literature and social anthropologists would be out of work.

Perhaps there is no underlying theme to provide a seamless understanding of this sculpture. Perhaps the medieval mind bounced from one statement about the world to another quite antipathetic one, in the same way that we get our kicks from channel surfing on TV. Watching someone switching from *The Simpsons* to *Live at the Met* to *Mr. Bean* might make a twelfth-century observer think the world had fallen into chaos; we, however, think this is selective viewing. In my ignorance, I have decided to settle for the opinion that the sculptural program here is a deliberate mixing of realism and fantasy.

Alongside the church is a big blooming profusion of flower stalls, all the flowers done up as bouquets ready for the giving. The church and the lady it honours are garlanded, so to speak, brilliantly. I can never get over the sight and scent of French flower stalls, the size and perfection of the blooms and the gorgeous multihued palette. It's easy to see where the stained-glass artists must have learned their colours, or were these flowers, later hybrids, inspired by church windows?

The interior of Nôtre-Dame is glorious. The height of the nave with its long lines of columns draws your attention directly to the sanctuary. There, a hemispherical group of marble columns surrounds the crowned figure of the Virgin, a golden girl with her babe on her lap, holding a stem of lilies in one hand, a set of keys in the other. The way the whole space works gives you the impression that she is a Greek goddess in a pantheon. With the capitals set on the columns less than a metre below the springing of the arches, which in turn support a palely frescoed dome, it is like being in a temple within a temple.

The unusual feeling of the place is carried over into the nave where, ever since the nineteenth century, the columns have been painted with unexciting geometric designs in muted decorator colours to blend with the stone. When Henry James saw this renovation he called it "the most hideous decorative painting that was ever inflicted upon passive pillars and indifferent vaults." My guidebook says that the sculptors Rodin and Bourdelle approved, however, thinking it brightened up the place. Henry would have been happy to learn that under the painted vaults lie remarkably beautiful eleventh-century frescoes that are gradually being uncovered from under the painting he loathed. What a joy to see them being brought to light, these iconic saints and angels, strong, even formidable, and yet gentle, their flowing curves and hieratic gestures showing their Byzantine ancestry. Something wonderful seems to be happening with their arrival: it is almost like the notion of Arthur's coming again when the country has need of him. We have need of these simple, certain images, no fussy curlicues, no fancy ways, just the straight goods.

It is in this great building that I am finally trapped into writing what has become this book. It is just before lunch, and wandering around the ambulatory I come to the central chapel of the apse, the one on the main axis of the church. Over this place, where they keep the Sacrament, there is a fine frescoed vault showing the crowning of the Virgin. Looking at this painting I am wondering once more why I need to write a book, instead of enjoying these riches for their own sake. At this moment the Angelus begins, and this tolling bell, which goes on forever, seems to be saying: Do it, do it. I try to persuade myself that it is saying: Stop it, stop it. Medieval people believed the world would end at high noon, so why shouldn't I quit at this moment? The notion won't stick. So, do it.

I'm not usually superstitious, nor overly sentimental, but I do believe in the sort of coincidence that somehow links up little cogs in a great wheel of being whose total circumference we will never know. That is probably just a more sophisticated version of your basic super-stitious nature. Whatever it is, I am convinced to carry on, at least till the next bell rings.

There are no flowers in the church. Strange that no one would carry a few inside, since they are sharing the lady's pavement outside. There is, however, a notice that says, "This church – like many others – was conceived as the earthly image of the heavenly world."

In such a space I begin to see what it is that we have lost. The idea of the holy, with its crucial complex of attraction and repulsion, of affect and awe, of love and terror, was once what drew people here and held them captive. The transcendent, the Holy One, was both present and beyond, invisible yet making himself known through symbols, of which this powerfully enclosing structure is one. In this place you could know that you are known, and know that the knowledge was true. You could fancy yourself, because of course approaching this deity was impossible really, touching the hem of majesty's cloak. Touch is perhaps the closest metaphoric act towards the divine; seeing, hearing and tasting are for the prophets and saints exclusively. Touching is for the boldest of the poor.

The church is more than an imitation of heaven. It is in itself, as symbol, a part of the real, the lasting, the constant. Today, as a model of heaven it has for me great aesthetic appeal, but only that. As a place of encounter, it clearly retains something of its earlier power. I feel it, I know some deep and moving truth remains, and that the mistake is only mine if I cannot uncover it.

Thinking back about this church and its predominant symbol, I realize how little I know or have cared about Mary. I have never been able to get past the humble, obedient aspect of her, though I am in love with countless representations of her, particularly sculptures where she seems to be so endearingly present. I have caught myself in museums and churches almost speaking to her, and then shaken myself for being so silly. Apart from this, she has never been my sort of woman.

Now I begin to wonder, how is it that the humble village girl was turned into a queen? What is it about her that made this transition possible? It is not a frog/prince kind of change. She must already have an inner spirit that could be exalted, so to speak. I think it is the devoted mother who is brought into centre stage, a mother whose relationship with her son is so unselfishly strong that she can ask favours of him, for others, not herself. For this nobility of character canonization by the church is not even enough; she is crowned by her son himself. I am sorry he did not crown Mary Magdalene too, but I guess you had to be pure (i.e., virginal) to begin with. I am beginning to wish I knew more about the cult of Mary. I know it arose very early in the fifth century, but of the circumstances I know nothing.

Mary has power, but it is restricted to the spiritual zone. She is part of the tree of Jesse, because the ancestry it illustrates is a sacred line, not just the usual knightly and therefore male progression. That is why the line can jump from Joseph over to Mary with no questions asked.

I eat my baguette lunch sitting on a wall outside Nôtre-Dame, then work it off going down a steep hill to find the Baptistery, the earliest extant Christian building in France. Cradle of French Christianity it was not, however: Christians have been worshipping in Lyons since AD 142. The central rectangular part of the baptistery was built in the fourth century, with an addition put on in the sixth. The early part holds the octagonal immersion pool, with steps going down into it, small and deep. The shape is modelled intentionally on the Roman mausoleum, to suggest death and rebirth. What pulsing emotions the ones about to be baptized might have had, going down into that pit, joyfully? timorously? both? And doing so knowing that the only way to come up was as a changed person committed to a strange new life. Mind you, Constantine had just made Christianity the established religion throughout the Empire, so one might have been baptized just because the boss said everyone in the stone yard or the weaving studio had to be. It would have been an unforgettable experience, all the same.

The early frescoes on these walls have been painted over in some places by more recent ones, thirteenth and fourteenth century, which makes them rather confusing. Those I can see clearly have a rhythmic grace that is utterly charming. Even the dragon facing off with a sword-brandishing knight has two flippant curls to his tail. For all its antiquity, the baptistery does not give off any sort of odour of sanctity, especially when a tour group of French grannies demonstrates that the acoustics in the place are just fine. I decide to go and visit the church of Sainte-Radegonde, the city's patron.

Radegonde's story, while grimmer than some, illustrates what options were open to women in the sixth century. These choices changed very little for hundreds of years. She was the daughter of King Herménéfride of Thuringia, whose kingdom was invaded by Clotaire, a nasty Merovingian king. Left behind with her brother while her father escaped (!), Radegonde, age ten, was taken home by Clotaire to be his bride. She refused to marry him, tried to escape, was brought back and forced to marry. After Clotaire assassinated her brother, she did get away successfully, and took the veil. Eventually she came to Poitiers where Clotaire, convinced by a miracle that he should let her go, helped her to build a convent.

Ruins of that convent lie near this church, part Romanesque, part Gothic, which stands on top of an earlier one constructed to house her tomb. According to the story of Radegonde that is told along the walls of the sacristy, she led a simple, pious life. At the same time, being well educated and intelligent, she drew a group of literary folk around her. St. Gregory of Tours, a good friend, renowned bishop and historian, officiated at her funeral and, says a contemporary account, "gave a very moving oration."

Although a convincing place of worship with the focal point its candlelit crypt, and a great frescoed vault above, the building says more to me about the continuation of ideas through time than it does about supernatural things. My heart is still with Radegonde, that poor kid whose father walked out on her. I am not surprised the city has taken to her; it seems to have a warm heart.

Some of the most horrific attitudes do not ever change, it seems. The Canadian newspaper *The Globe and Mail* carried a report recently that a Moslem woman was stoned to death for trying to leave Afghanistan with a man who was not a relative. Radegonde fared better. The two accounts indicate the same woman-as-chattel belief, as laundered through a rigid religious ethic. Both Islam and Christianity have a great deal to answer for.

Is it necessary for all belief systems to be so nastily exclusive in order to survive? To convince ourselves of our rightness, our chosen status, all the others must be damned, even if they are the wives, daughters, children of those doing the condemning. Then, to resolve the inner ambivalence men must have about this, they reclassify women as baggage, necessary to produce more men, and sometimes thought to be soulless and therefore outside the salvation program. In a recent issue of the *International Herald Tribune* I noticed an item that said an ambassador had given a speech in a light vein entitled "Have Women Souls?" Shocked, I looked more carefully, and saw it was an item quoted from an edition of the paper of seventy-eight years ago. But why, of all the items the paper could have reprinted, was this the one chosen? I am still shocked. The idea is not so far behind us as to be the subject of humour. I am speculating as to the gender of the editor of this page. Anyway, even in 1922 the subject was no longer relevant. It was decided once and for all by the Council of Trent in 1563 that women did have souls.

Poitiers certainly has a keenness for sacred history of all sorts. Over a coffee, I pick up the local paper, which reminds me that the 28th of September is St. Wenceslas' day. Born 907; died 929, assassinated by his brother. His colour is blue, his number seven. One of the local restaurants offers a business card with a calendar on the back listing the saints-du-jour. Another news item in the daily says that the previous day the Order of St. Fortunatus gave a cheque for 10,000 francs to the city to help with new works. The order is concerned with the environment, and with good relations among different peoples. The writer comments on the importance of holding this meeting in Poitiers, because Fortunatus, AD 535–609, was bishop of Poitiers, and it was he who wrote the life of Radegonde, patron saint of this city. How long this sort of remembering will last is a good question: in the accompanying photo, none of the members of the order looks under eighty. The paper also carries an announcement of tonight's concert in honour of the nine-hundredth anniversary of Saint-Jean de Montierneuf, a former Cluniac abbey. I go. The music is from the ninth to the thirteenth centuries, Gregorian, antiphonal, polyphonic, the stuff to set me meditating on the history of God in this place. I am happy to note that the age span of the capacity audience is well under eighty.

The next day is another strenuous walking day. I want to see the dolmen, the prehistoric standing stone, on the hill across the river, proof that the city was inhabited in 3000 BC, and also a Merovingian tomb nearby. The guard at the museum on this side of the Clain suggests I go on foot, ten minutes, he says. The woman who gives me directions says fifteen, since the hill is quite steep. It is. I make it in twenty, struggling all the way up in the heat, and stop to rest under the beneficent gold arm of the statue of Our Lady of the Dunes. She may have blessed my route, but not my arrival. After further instructions from a policeman at the *gendarmerie*, I walk some more, only to find the gate to the tomb's grounds locked. I am not the only one disappointed: I agree with the other visitors that this closing is unusual. Then, exhausted, having looked vainly for the dolmen, I go down the hill a shorter, steeper way, and find a bench in a lovely little park along the Clain.

Here the river slides along gently bearing its cargo of crumpling yellow leaves and convoys of ducks, parents in the lead giving the most raucous cries. "Keep up, Willie! Practise your strokes!" I can't help thinking that my fruitless excursion was another life-is-like simile: a strenuous effort followed by a grateful rest, and a need to summarize: Where have I been? To what end? Was it worth it? Today, my aching toes say it was hardly worth it, but every other part of me says, yes. This whole journey isn't just about the satisfaction of arrival, but about going there, and later on, the recollections in tranquillity. All of these make up the full experience that I want from life, and that give it its meaning. I'll see that dolmen in reality one day. For now I have pictures and stories.

This ancient landmark, called "la Pierre-Levée," the raised stone, is a tablestone supported on three pillars that must have taken tremendous strength and effort to put in place. The people of Poitiers have two different explanations for how it got there. The old tradition says that the fairy-goddess Mélusine carried the various parts of the standing stone in her apron. The new one says that St. Radegonde brought the table on her head, the pillars in her apron. Unfortunately, as she bent her head to put the table top down, the devil stole one of the four pillars; that is why it stands on only three. Christians: 3, Old Nick: 1.

I am not surprised at the way these contests usually turned out. Mélusine is a Celtic figure, the patron of Parthenay, about 50 kilometres away from Poitiers, and of nearby Lusignan, whose noble family claimed descent from her. Because she is both a pre-Christian figure and a protector of other neighbouring groups, she had to be bested by the saint. In the second story, the only possible explanation for a three-footed table is the devil's activity.

Mélusine is not simply dealt with as a pagan phantasm, however. Writers tried to make a would-be Christian out of her: a fairy who wants to be a mortal. The problem is, she is too powerful, too primordially compelling to make her into either a human or a fluttering fairy. The bare outline of the tale shows why. To avenge her mother for her father's breaking his oath, Mélusine shuts up papa inside a mountain. Mother in fury curses her: her legs will turn into a serpent's tail every Saturday night. No one is supposed to know, so when her jealously suspicious husband peeks and sees the transformation, Mélusine has to disappear. She sprouts wings and flies off, rattling the château as she goes, and leaving her ten sons behind (although she comes back to nurse the youngest).

A contemporary pilgrim who copied this story into his notebook last year included the narrator's remark that if women sometimes seem a bit viperish, it's because they are descended from Mélusine. He dismisses the legend as false. "Normally, it is impossible that our gentle companions should hide venom in their breasts with which to kill men." His denial betrays him: it's not venom, but there is a sudden warmth coursing through my bloodstream when I read lines like that.

Here's another sex scandal just like the Eve-serpent-God one, only here it's Mélusine/serpent-Mum. Adam and Mélusine's husband are both voyeurs; the parents are both angry at the women. The latter are mythical equivalents of the serpent, and both together represent sexual knowledge, probably of androgyny and the separation that came afterwards. Mélusine's story, and perhaps originally Adam and Eve's, embodies the idea of the equality of the sexes, and the understanding of the masculine/feminine complex that inheres in all of us.

Here in Poitiers and vicinity are the stories of two women, Radegonde and Mélusine, who were victims of patriarchal thinking and yet accomplished things of some size and significance. Radegonde established her convent and her circle of savants. Mélusine performed prodigious feats, including building the château at Lusignan overnight, and protecting and warning her erstwhile family and city of danger – to this day? I didn't inquire.

Finally I am ready to seek out my original goal. At the other side of the city, close to the river Boivre, is the basilica of Saint-Hilaire, the shrine visited by medieval pilgrims, and others before that. Hilaire became a Christian when he was middle-aged, sometime after Constantine declared that the civilized world was going to put away its old gods in favour of the One, and was made the first (so it is thought) bishop of Poitiers. He was a scholar, an orthodox theologian who wrote on the doctrine of the Trinity at the time when the great Arian heresy, claiming that God had created Jesus whom he later raised to divine status, had taken control of the minds of the powers-that-be. For his position he was exiled, and spent several years in the east, studying the church in Greece and Turkey. Eventually he made his point, and managed to get some Arian bishops thrown out of the church in Gaul. He was a dynamic defender of the faith whose name is still attached to the third term of the university year in England. I am eager to see the building that honours this fighting saint.

From the outside it has the look that's now familiar of a goodly Romanesque pilgrimage church: the ample apsidial east end, chapels topped by the ambulatory which is topped by a dome, the whole thing a balanced perfection of curved spaces and modest buttresses. That's the best view. The setting is unprepossessing: a small garden pulls you around to the front door, which has almost no open space before it, the church being squeezed in by a laneway separating it from a school next door. It doesn't matter, because the façade is not much to look at; too many generations have played around with it. Quite certain about what I will find inside, a sound, rational space with perhaps some curious elements, I go in.

I know I said something out loud, probably *"Mon Dieu!"* which in the circumstances wasn't intended at all profanely. Here is one of the most impressive interiors I've ever seen. The last time I remember being so astonished was at Vézelay, my first-ever Romanesque building.

It's not so very beautiful, it's too busy for that. It's vast, stretching in all directions, but mainly up. I realized later that the church is built on the hillside, making it structurally necessary to have ascending levels. Going forward from the door along a broad side aisle you go up, not by slight rises, but by steps that take you up about two metres or more to the next level where the altar sits, and then another three metres to the ambulatory. At this point you have arrived in a space the size of a small theatre. It must have been one, because it held the crowds of relic-seeking pilgrims who came to honour St. Hilaire's bones. Perhaps they were on display in the apse then; today the relics, if indeed they are the saint's bones and not someone else's, are in a case inside a casket behind a grille in the inaccessible crypt. Somehow I can't help thinking of Walter M. Miller Jr.'s 1959 anti-utopian novel *A Canticle for Leibowitz*, where the monks revered the ancient shopping list ("can kraut, six bagels – bring home for Emma") found in a bomb shelter, and disregarded the fine illuminated copy one of the brothers had made.

Most Romanesque churches, within the first hundred years of their lives, had replaced their wooden beamed roofs with stone, usually because fire had taken the original. Here the builder decided to create three domes over the nave, a huge, weighty undertaking. To do this, he added a set of columns for support, and linked them to the existing columns between nave and aisles with small arches. That's why the building seems to march on and on, one's eye confused by so many columns. It's not a detriment, though, since on a very dull, chill day, the stone is warm, welcoming, even embracing. With its domes and crypt it has visually and psychologically a feminine aspect. Besides, the church has no teeth – no savagery is apparent, no hint of pressing guilt and gnawing punishment.

As the pilgrims ascended up and up their eyes must have opened in amazement at the sight of the panoply of frescoes, many covered over today, but whose restoration has been underway since the last century. I found St. Martin in the act of slicing his cloak in two with his sword, the beggar standing in his boxers already grasping his half. The next panel is a mandorla showing Christ, his arms wide as he blesses St. Martin for his kindness. The colours are pale ochre and orange-red with a deeper raw umber made glorious springtime by a lively fresh green background. In another fresco, St. George, with what seem to be aerodynamically correct wings, is threatening a sassy dragon with perky ears, a lolling tongue and wings best saved for heraldry, not flying.

The building takes my breath away, it is so solemn, so truthful. For a pilgrim such as myself, this is the place to rest, to stay, and if possible to return. I am in love, but with what? With what it tells me: that I wasn't wrong to set my heart on the Christian hope for the world; that it is related to something beyond itself, perhaps no more certain about what that is than I am, though seeming so. These stones touch me powerfully. They have stood for something for a very long time; they are not meaningless cut rocks. Over time they have been painted, chiselled, plastered over and patched. Still they're there, composing a whole that is greater than the sum of them.

A young man comes in, walks the route of the saints around the ambulatory, returns to sit for a while, perhaps just as surprised as I am. People worship and pray here. It shows. There is one of those thank-you-for-favours-received tablets that you see everywhere in the chapels of French churches. This one says simply, "This church has been my light and my peace. H.C. 1909."

I leave the church, determined to come back for mass the next day, and find myself a table in the lovely eighteenth-century park nearby in order to drink coffee and think about what I've seen. I am slowing down, thanks to this city. Not slow by nature, I have to tell myself it's all right to stay for three hours in Saint-Hilaire, to walk all day, to take all the time I want. It's also all right not to finish what I set out to do, cover this city from end to end. Better to be led by feeling, intuition or whatever.

Behind me in conversation with the waiter, a friend says, "*Il n'y a pas de quoi du bon.*" Nothing's any good. I disagree. *Il y a beaucoup de bon.*

At the next day's mass I am surprised to find the church so full with people of all ages, except young children. Everything has changed so much since I last attended a service in France. There is no kneeling; you stand to pray. The priests face the people at a very plain, modern altar table a few feet away from the front row of chairs. There is plenty of singing in small snippets throughout, led by the choir director who pops up to conduct almost as often as the priest speaks. Women participate a lot: conducting the choir, leading the prayers, reading, bringing up the bread and wine – everything but saying the magic words, as my clerical friends put it.

I am not much taken with the music. We sing simple, folky tunes that everyone can manage. The volunteer choir isn't bad, although if it really is Duruflé they are singing as a motet, they murder it. A budding organist gives us a short Bach piece rather tremulously, but it is good to listen to in that ringing place. Actually, everything is very suitable, and not the least esoteric. In this building and with this type of worship, a Mozart mass would have been an odd invasion of taste.

Is there still some sense of mystery here? Yes, but it's not spooky. It's neither remote nor centred upon one image. Everything here matters. Everything is central. I am in the mystery. It is so very twentieth century, this feeling, yet I think I owe it all to these ancient stones. That's the difference between Nôtre-Dame and Saint-Hilaire; in the former it is the Virgin who is the focus, while here it is the setting, the whole. That's why it is more world-focussed. The church is theatrical, intending to show that this world is the true theatre. Believing this, I recall that St. Hilaire raised people from the dead. If they were better off after death, why would he have bothered?

This is the place for me, for contemplation, for infusion of new energy, anticipating a new focus. It doesn't solve any of my problems with theology, with the institutional church's reactionary attitudes, but I believe it could do so in time, were I able to stay long enough. I will return; I know it will do me much good to do so.

Turning my back on Saint-Hilaire is hard because now that I have worshipped there it has risen to the top of my Romanesque chart. It has given me something of its inwardness. Poitiers, for many reasons including this one, is my first four-star pilgrimage city. Even those not on any particular trail, past or present, would love it, I'm sure.

I've been wondering about the connection between women and pilgrimage. Women went, of course, both high- and low-born, and, while the majority of pilgrims would have been men, it nevertheless seems like a feminine sort of pursuit. In the old moral conflict of means versus ends, it usually happens that men will argue that one may use almost any means to obtain a goal provided it produces a good result in the end. (There are limits, of course, but the line is drawn at a different place than it is by most women.) Women are more likely to take the opposite position, saying that no end, however laudatory, justifies the use of (in their view) unjust, harmful or cruel means. The argument may devolve into a discussion of what is truly just, harmful, etc. – which is the way to make sure the woman always loses, by making unresolvable metaphysical questions the issue instead of ethics.

I am sure that a large part of the reason for this ethical gender division is because most women are not strategists. It is not that they are incapable, or that they would not like to be, but because they have not had the training up till now. Few women play chess, for instance. I am a pathetic player, easily defeated. The closest I ever came to the tactics of warfare was on the archery range at camp. Now there's a particularly relevant twentieth-century practice! I learned nothing about the strategy into which this might fit, because there is no such thing today.

According to Shakespeare, Richard III was bored and useless when there was no war to fight, so he turned to crime, in which he showed himself a consummate strategist until he became king. Women, on the other hand, concentrate on the quality of life, the means to an end, because they are fed up with their failure to achieve grand goals, or because it never even occurred to them that they might have them. With some notable exceptions (including, as we will see, this city's famous Eleanor), they simply have not known how to carry on any vast project that takes strategic planning.

All this is changing as women begin to grasp the implications of what has been denied them, or what they themselves believed was neither possible nor virtuous. When I was teaching I used to get pretty fed up with some of my male colleagues, who remarked on how aggressive I was. Had I been a man they wouldn't have noticed, as I acted pretty much the way they did, except that I'm no strategist. I'm fairly good at carrying out short-term goals, but I always want to take in too many conflicting considerations or qualifications to be able to bring off larger ones. For these I need the help of those who can put the goal clearly and firmly into context. They are usually men. A pity, but it's true.

In the light of these ideas, much of Protestantism seems so masculine. Stripped down, it says avoid becoming entangled in the delights of this world, which distract you from God, and head for the goal which is achieved much later, in the hereafter. Protestantism is firmly monotheistic. The means to the goal is by negation, subduing your will, doing your duty, controlling your passions, even blocking out your senses. My Presbyterian forebears took this path cheerfully and faithfully.

Catholicism, however you rationalize it, seems somewhat polytheistic. Saints and miracles abound everywhere. This mentality has toned down a lot since the thirteenth century, but it is still there. People still walk to the saints. Going on a pilgrimage in which all the stages, byways and detours are parts of the sacred means shows how, in one hugely important project, the feminine approach had its way.

One of the buildings I would love to have seen doesn't exist anymore, but it is magnificently illustrated on the July page of the *Très Riches Heures* of the duc de Berry. About 1375 the duc constructed a glistening white triangular fortified château at the confluence of the two rivers: the Boivre and the Clain. He built it while he was waiting for the workmen to finish the renovations on Eleanor's old palace, and needed somewhere to live. Amplified with gardens containing pools of swans, it must have been enchanting. Jean duc de Berry was an aesthete, bringing to his court artists, architects and the three brothers Limbourg, the miniaturists who were responsible for the *Très Riches Heures* and the *Belles Heures*. He also commissioned his librarian to write the story of Mélusine, the one we have today.

I keep wondering about the triangular shape of the château. It can't have been for lack of space. Was it done to be avant-garde, or to imitate the shape of the isthmus? Or was it to represent the Trinity? An unlikely thought. It's lighter and more palace-like than a square or oblong; perhaps that was the idea. Two mouldering remnants of towers are all that are left of this fairytale building. Ah well, today it might have been a B & B. We have the illumination still.

Although Poitiers' patron saint is Radegonde, its patron is Eleanor of Aquitaine. It was her favourite city, to which she came between her marriages to Louis VII of France and Henry Plantagenet, and for another spell when she was setting up her sons to challenge Henry. It was from here that she launched her son Richard as future duke, thus making sure that Henry would have no excuse to grab her lands, should she die before him.

There seem to have been two ways to avoid being mistreated if you were a woman: the possession of property or virginity. Eleanor was legally free to manage her own duchy and its lineage. When she came close to treason against Henry, he treated her as a prisoner of war and noble rival, not as a truant wife. She was too powerful for that. Radegonde, on the other hand, lost her property in war, and so had to resort to the only thing left to her, her virginity.

Even if you came from royal stock, unless you held property in your own right you could be in big trouble. The worst example of heir-lust and bad faith I have read is the story of Lothaire, one of Charlemagne's weak and rotten sons. Lacking an heir by his wife Teutberge, he wanted, as the biblical expression was, to put her away in favour of his concubine who had produced three sons already. Pope Hadrian II wouldn't approve of taking the interdict against divorce so lightly; he had his people torture the queen to force a confession of misbehaviour from her. Then Lothaire could divorce her for adultery, and the church could stand righteously on its principles.

The pope's behaviour isn't all that out of line with his people's. It was taken for granted that all women, being incorrigibly and incessantly lustful, were likely to look for satisfaction beyond the marriage bed after they had exhausted their husbands. The only virgins in society were outside it, in convents. It must be so, feminine nature being what it was. The only chaste woman, and certainly the only married virgin, was Mary. There is a horrendous example of doublethink in the story of a girl who, when pursued by an ardent canon, refused to give up her virginity for fear of damnation. The rejected lover (would-be rapist?) reasoned that if she was so obstinate she must be a heretic, most likely one of the Cathars. He denounced her. As Georges Duby says, "She was arrested. She was judged. The proof was incontestable. She was burned."

Eleanor's reputation suffered badly towards the end of her life and particularly after her death. Chroniclers being for the most part in the pay of ecclesiastical or royal contenders, no one seems to know what degree of truth there is in these stories, or whether there is any at all. She is accused of being an adulteress, a sorceress who caused sterility in Louis. Well, not quite, since they had two daughters, but that wasn't what he needed to continue the Capetian line. She is accused of incest with her uncle, and of allowing herself to be seduced by a Saracen noble while on crusade in Jerusalem against these very infidels. People associated her and her four warlike sons with the viperish Mélusine, whose eight out of ten sons were physically grotesque. The revered Cistercian, St. Bernard, quotes Richard the Lion Heart, Eleanor's favourite son, as saying, "It is not surprising that we brothers fight, since we are the offspring of the devil."

Duby says that the reasons for such bad press are, first, that she is a woman, so what could you expect? Second, that her grandfather was a lecher and not a nice man. Third, that the church had just ruled that marriage is one of the seven sacraments and eternally binding, and she was divorced. Finally, that she had incited her sons to rebellion against Henry. With the powers of church and kingdom against her, and such indisputable logic, not to mention the monks' view of women, no wonder there were few good words spoken of her. I'd love to know what she was really like.

Despite the strength of women in this town, I find no models to adapt for twentieth-century life. They all seem to have a problem with power, the use or absence of it. There is Mary, whose only power is to act as a channel to a higher one. Radegonde is powerless to choose her own destiny. She takes the only safe profession available to her, in which she makes a rich and admirable life for herself and others. Mélusine is ultimately deprived of her goal – marriage – yet uses what power she has left to help others. She is rather like Radegonde, but, I think, even more frustrated because she is robbed of her chance to use her abilities well. Eleanor goes from reigning queen, to prisoner, to effective ruler after Henry dies. She is powerful, aggressive, probably clever, and just as likely unloved, though it is hard to know, given such biased biographers.

Is there always to be a trade-off between love and power? At the ideal level no, but it is hard to achieve even high-minded goals without using people as instruments rather than enjoying them for their own sakes. Mary is an instrument: is she really loved? Perhaps. Is it power-lessness that causes women to acquire other virtues? I think this is partly true. Would women run the state or the church better than men if they had the power? I doubt it. Public virtue would have to change in order to make any great difference. The problem may also be that women who have achieved power still think like men, and that is how they made it. Will women bishops make any difference to the ways of my church? I guess that to answer that I need to know whether they consider and subscribe to any feminist theological thinking. Without some change of thought, how can the social structure that is the church be changed? Or must the direction come, as it usually does, from society first? The questions are too difficult for me to do more than raise them. In the meantime I'm not holding my breath waiting for a good marriage between love and power.

CHAPTER 5

— AULNAY, FLARAN —

Peter. *Saint. b? in Galilee province, Palestine?; d? Rome. Fisherman. Called by Jesus to be one of his twelve followers, and later to be the founder of the church that bears his name. Missionary, preacher, healer.*

Bernard of Clairvaux. *Saint. b. circa 1089, Fontaines, Burgundy; d. 1153, Clairvaux. First abbot of Cistercian abbey of Clairvaux. Preacher of the Second Crusade, adviser to kings and popes, founder of abbeys. Fought heresy strenuously, against Peter Abelard and against the Cathars. Received visitations from the Virgin Mary.*

The church of Saint-Pierre-de-la-Tour sits on the edge of the insignificant town of Aulnay, population 1,500, just where you get on the highway to Saintes. It was actually built outside the town walls, right on the pilgrims' route to Santiago de Compostela. Today people such as myself, making a deliberate detour to see the church, might wonder as they drive towards its dismal surroundings why they are bothering, until they reach the actual site. We parked the car and got out, and there it was across the road, completely visible: an unassuming stone church, all alone in its churchyard, a simple, perfect form.

Originally a Benedictine abbey built in the twelfth century, it later passed into the hands of the canons of Poitiers cathedral until the Revolution. Art historians praise it, and its portals appear in many books on Romanesque art, but it is hard to tell whether it is much favoured today as a place of worship or even tourism. Bob and I had the church to ourselves the first afternoon we went there, and only a couple of people joined us the second time. We were free to explore and come to cherish it for its humble, extraordinary beauty.

We began examining it carefully at the east end where the apse, a pirouette of hemicircles perfectly balanced, is adorned with what appear to me to be Celtic designs. There is a carved band, called a string course, of horses eating each others' tails. Below the window horses fly, strange beasts munch, but delicately, in keeping with the serenity and order of the building. Other medallions show workers who seem to be engaged in building the church. From under the overhang of the roof a wonderful assortment of heads, animal and human, peers down at us. I couldn't stop taking pictures. Every group of figures, every angle, every perspective was one I wanted to remember. Although it sounds cluttered, the effect is harmonious and simple. In a way, the apse is enough in itself; even if the rest of the building were a misfit, it wouldn't matter. The church has given plenty.

The architecture of this region, Saintonge, has some stylistic elements peculiar to itself, as has Poitou, the region around Poitiers. Aulnay mixes both, particularly in the doorways, with the series of graduated archivolts, carved arches, leading the eye and the understanding towards the interior of the church. The door on the south side is massive and yet un-intimidating in its size. On each of the four archivolts that act as a funnel to draw you inside, a range of figures illustrates a theme. You can see the twelfth-century clerical mind at work: the outer rim shows the animals both familiar and strange and who are not yet redeemed; the next shows the twenty-four elders on the eve of the final judgment day; the next shows the saints and apostles, already redeemed; and in the inner ring are six griffins who here represent Christ. The sacred hierarchy has been clearly laid out on the outside before you take a single step inside the building, where the way of salvation will be illustrated for you in various visual and aural ways.

The façade of the church is off-centre, making the tower seem misplaced too, which it isn't. The building's supposedly matching elements do not: the two sets of pillars are dissimilar in height, width and shape. The blind arcades, the same in design, are different widths, and part of one is covered up by a pillar. The gables, one at each end of the roof, do match, though the slope of the roof is different on each side. What seemed at first to be the tiny perfect church turns out to be quite imperfect. The overall effect is so integrated it took me two visits to notice this imbalance.

In the interior, pilgrims would find solace in the simplicity, the fine proportions and the gift of light coming through the lantern, the transept window and the open south door. The animals are here again, mythic and marauding, chewing each other and humans. Over the north transept there is a frieze with a virgin, a demon, a griffin, a menacing cat-figure, a demon. To a twentieth-century eye it seems like the prototype for the mixed metaphor.

In fact, the beasts and the demons have me flummoxed. Why are there such combinations of the noble and the gruesome? Did people really believe in these creatures? Surely they weren't for entertainment. How did they fit into the salvation story? Searching about for help on these questions I have found several opinions, none of which really explain everything. Most art historians want to tell you from whence, but never how come.

Dante suggests that there are four levels of meaning to a narrative. Similarly, four types of explanation have been given for these figures. On the literal level, one source says these fabulous animals are taken from travellers' mistaken tales of what they saw in strange places. He says also that some of these designs are Mesopotamian in origin, which actually gives him two arguments. Then he states that there is a similarity to the iconography because the artists moved about, copying designs they saw on their travels. That gives him a third explanation, unless we assume that all the travellers were artists who went to Mesopotamia and made lots of mistakes.

On the allegorical level there is the view that animals were combined into new and more powerful creatures in order to represent desired qualities, hence the griffin which is part eagle, part lion. Animals, usually the known varieties, also appeared as attributes of the saints. The swan was Mary, the white stag Jesus, and of course we have the lion for St. Mark, the eagle for St. John, and so on.

On Dante's third, moral level, we have the argument that figures that are part human, part beast were satanic, and intended to terrorize the unwilling into good behaviour.

Finally at the top of the heap there is the theological view put forward by Davy, writing on Romanesque symbolism, that all creation, including the pagan figures of antiquity, can be subsumed into Christ who is past, present and future.

That's the capsule version of my digging, and none of this quite holds water. Gurevich puts it all together in his wonderful analysis of the grotesque through medieval documents, but that's going to have to wait until another moment.

I realize, in looking so intently and delightedly at this stunning church, that I am treating it as art, and as a frozen piece of history. It is a stimulus to thought, but not, by any means, the prayerful place it was built to be. I give it less than its due. One of the problems in writing all this down is the detachment it brings: not the detachment that lets you critique your own work, but that separates you from lived experience. I ask myself now, is this what I really think? Is this the person I really am, or am I making up a persona for this book, some-one who perhaps sounds better than she is – or maybe worse – but certainly not the same? And if I am making up a fictional Anne, what is happening meantime to my life? Am I learning and living in parallel with what I'm writing, or do I lag behind, slip away?

Reading Robert Lowell, whose writing on poetry almost rivals his poetry itself, I discovered this shadowy question lurking at the back of my mind. In discussing Gerard Manley Hopkins, he draws this con-trast: "When we examine Pope, Wordsworth, Coleridge, Arnold, or Browning, I think we realize that after a certain point all these men – all of them great writers at times and highly religious in their fashion – stopped living; they began to reflect, to imagine, to moralize: some single faculty kept on moving and fanning the air, but the whole man had stopped."

Am I merely fanning the air? Right now while I am trying to think and write and be on pilgrimage, there is always that nagging question: why don't I just go and do it?

In defence of this task, sometimes there is a reversal of – what shall I call it? – commitment perhaps, when it seems that I find myself closer to the deep heart's core in the writing than in the activity about which I write. All the distractions of wandering around these sites, like the rough cobblestones, the dog caca, the abruptly shrinking sidewalks when you find yourself with one foot on the road, and the sense of displacement mean that I have to concentrate on the immediate prat-falls rather than ultimate ones. Then when I am back at home, sitting at the desk or on the terrace watching nothing more complex than the horizon line, I find the sense of all the previous patchwork coming together. Then I know where and why I've been.

Though this church was built when there was no separation of art from religion, when art was, as Duby says, the means of perpetuating and remembering rituals, it is no longer so. Once you have become self-conscious about art, or about God for that matter, it becomes, in McLuhan's phrase, anti-environment, to be noticed, studied, analyzed. I guess it cannot be helped. I shall continue to explore this gem of a building.

Outside again, the main west door is similar in design, although not as magnificent, as the south portal. The figures are set parallel to the lines of the archivolt, instead of at right angles, making them seem to be sleeping or at least more relaxed. There is nothing casual about the other doorway element, however, the blind arcades on each side of the door framing life-size stone figures. In the arcade on the left St. Peter, the abbey's patron, is shown being crucified upside down.

The sight of this jolts me out of my art phase. The idea is gruesome, and sets up all kinds of unpleasant vibrations in me. I remember the story that Peter, deeply remorseful that he had denied knowing Jesus during his trial, requested this form of crucifixion, saying that he did not deserve to die in the same way as his Lord. Notwithstanding his cowardly behaviour and his feelings about it, why does the church decide to commemorate this event, to face everyone with it as they come inside to consider their own relationship to God? Peter has another formidable side: he is the one to whom Jesus gave the job of founding the church. It is clear by the time this church was built that he has done the job well. Then why single out his weakest moment? This is the dark side of Christianity, the self-flagellation, the masochism that is being emphasized. If the church can reveal the great underbelly of our lives, and then correct and comfort it, we will be devotees for life. Look at Peter.

I cannot stomach this attitude, which has for the most part disappeared from the present-day theology I know, though I think it lurks in some sectarian corners still. I wish it were not part of the otherwise lovely fabric that is Saint-Pierre of Aulnay.

There's another dark patch here, though of a different sort. Surrounding the church is the cemetery, a scene of crumbling desolation and seeming destructiveness. Coffin-shaped stones rest on plinths, or at least they used to. Almost all the stones are in disarray, knocked off their plinths, broken in pieces, or stood casually against others that have no apparent relationship to them. Some are upside down. What caused this devastation, this neglect? Not a flower, plastic or living, brightens this place, not a picture of the beloved, an obligatory element in any French cemetery. Where are the devoted families to tend these graves?

None of the inscriptions are fully legible, but in reading such dates as I could, another mystery appeared: everyone whose epitaph I read had died in the same year, 1865. I discovered from the guide booklet that these were the graves of legionnaires, but found no information as to where they died, and why they were buried here en masse. Just as strange is the lack of more recent burials. We wandered the whole cemetery and found only three tombstones dated in this century.

The sadness of the cemetery has affected me. The cypresses standing ten metres tall above the tombstones seem poor protectors.

Five children found us picnicking on the gravestones. *"Anglais?"* (with excitement) *"Non, Canadiens."* (disappointment, then second thoughts:) *"Ah, arrêtez!"* and took our picture, each one peeking around the cypresses to snap a quick one. Rare beasts for their collection.

The idea of detachment is in my mind as I leave Aulnay for Flaran. It certainly appears there in its most extreme form, abandonment. Peter's abandonment of Jesus, the church's and families' abandonment of the graves: both are a withdrawal of love for the formerly beloved, leaving a vacuum, a moral and emotional loss. It is the kind of detachment I worry about when I become an art pilgrim, afraid it may mean that I am ceasing to be a real one.

Detachment takes on an entirely different character when I come to Flaran, a former Cistercian abbey in Gascony, northwest of Toulouse. It is just a stone's throw off the pilgrims' western route to Spain, close to several other major shrines; but the way of Christian living it espouses is far removed from that which produced the idea of pilgrimage.

There are two distinctly French kinds of religious sensibility; I want to call them Cluniac and Cistercian after the great monastic orders. The monks of Cluny are the great travel agents of the Middle Ages. They are the ones who encouraged the idea of going on pilgrimages, who set up hostels, had bridges built, warned pilgrims of the dangers of the route, and even provided a guidebook for the route to Santiago de Compostela. They built churches designed to take the crowds who came through the towns along the route to venerate the relics of locally enshrined saints. Early on, their success as sponsors of pilgrimages was ensured when one of the abbots of Cluny managed to acquire the ashes of both saints Peter and Paul for the motherhouse. By the year 1100 the monks of Cluny had over fourteen hundred monasteries and abbeys under their care. They became immensely wealthy, and some of their finest buildings stand today as a testament to the good taste that money could buy: Sacré-Coeur at Paray-le-Monial near the motherhouse, Sainte-Foy at Conques, Saint-Pierre at Moissac, the Madeleine at Vézelay, and of course Santiago de Compostela at the end of the long, arduous road. The massive abbey church at Cluny, constructed between 1088 and 1130, was the largest church in Christendom until St. Peter's basilica was built in Rome.

I don't mean to put my tongue in my cheek in speaking this way about the well-endowed religious. Putting aside the fact that we know all motives are mixed, I think that they had an important insight into the way spirituality can blossom and increase in the inner person. They believed, as I do, that life is a pilgrimage from start to finish. The main distinction between the larger form and the microcosmic ones, like my travels to the saints, is that in the latter the routes are fairly clearly marked out for one to follow, or deviate from, or turn around and go back where you came from. In life there aren't any routes, only the occasional guidepost, and you certainly cannot go home again if you don't like where you are. Here is where the symbols of the pilgrimage and the wilderness meet. The wilderness may have many paths through it, but to find the one that is yours is no easy matter. Most of the time I'm not sure whether I've got it right for me or not; I don't know if I'll ever find that out. Once in a while there is a little part of the track that seems exactly right to take, but perhaps even hindsight will not tell me whether it was.

The Cluniacs, in the Platonic spirit of "as in heaven, so on earth," said that walking to the saints *was* walking to the saints. These aren't images of saints, they are real, fully alive in their new and wonderful afterlife, which is occurring even now. Hence, their approachability and helpfulness. (This idea is rather like the Buddhist figure of the Bodhisattva who has achieved enlightenment and then returns after death to teach and encourage the rest of us.) In the old controversy about the efficacy of faith versus works in achieving one's appropriate heavenly reward, the Cluniacs were for faith, believing that praise, prayer, study and meditation and especially the veneration of relics were the best way. Not that they were against good works; they had the hostels and hospitals to prove it. It was that they sought the glory of God by looking heavenward, and going on pilgrimage was one sure way of reaching for glory.

I suppose the monks of Cluny would roughly correspond to sociologist Max Weber's "inner-worldly mystic" type. They advocated pilgrimage for the laity and secular clergy, though not for themselves, who stayed in their abbeys engaged in intellectual and contemplative pursuits.

The Cistercians are quite another type, the "other-worldly ascetic," who, following the example of the second-century Desert Fathers, built their monasteries far from any madding crowds, in forests, on hilltops, in order to have as little as possible to do with society. Their watchwords are prayer, silence, abstinence and manual labour, not thought, as they necessarily had to spend much of their time raising food and keeping themselves equipped with necessities. They adhered to the ideal of a community in the wilderness, but not to the pilgrimage. Their great leader, St. Bernard of Clairvaux, said, "Man does not know that the centre of the pilgrimage is his own heart. That is why he leaves his country, hoping to find the place where heaven and earth are joined." Although they believed in renouncing the world themselves, nevertheless they did provide hostels for pilgrims. I suppose along many of those wild routes the Cistercian houses were literally the only beacons of light and warmth. Ironically, today one of their fine legacies, the abbey of Flaran, is a centre for Compostela studies.

The Cistercians have always had a great appeal for me, because of their unflinching dedication and seeming purity of purpose. All their abbeys that I have visited, Fontvrauld, Fontenay and Sénanque, are beautiful in their simplicity, their order, their control and understanding of volumes of space. So I came with high hopes to Flaran.

It is set like a grand château at the end of a straight *allée* outlined by trees, giving the impression of being a larger establishment than it actually is. The building is well restored, the stonework clean, solid and orderly, just as one would expect from a Cistercian building. Inside the fence that ties together buildings and courtyard, all the ingredients of the monastic plan are there: the church; and the cloister, off which are the chapter room, *chauffoir* (the only heated room for winter comfort) and refectory. The sleeping area or *dortoir* is upstairs, connected to the church itself by a stairway. There would be no excuse to be late for prayers here. This tight, trim design meant that, as a medieval writer put it, "here the sheep are kept as in a fold." Bernard called a monastery a prison with open gates.

In the proper fashion, we were led into this complex through the former guest wing, and thence into the church. There's no doubt, it is lovely, this fair, open space empty of decoration or architectural fuss. There are no distractions; only the light of heaven comes in from the clear windows. There is nothing hidden, no ambulatory with saints in chapels and niches, no crypt, no relics. You face the altar and concentrate on the one thing necessary, addressing and listening to God. St. Bernard says, "The Name of Jesus has the taste of honey in the mouth," which really expresses what these monks took delight in. Bernard believed that silence and light were the proper symbols of God.

I wish the joy and delight were still present today, but for me they weren't. It was a ghost of a building, of an ideal; whatever was real about it had slipped away. All I could say was, I knew it had been there once, and how sorry I was to have missed it. As we went through the rest of the buildings, empty and open to the outdoors, the impression grew firmer. I had expected that: empty rooms anywhere are sad places, robbed of human living. In one room off the cloister there was an exhibition of sculpture, clippings, photographs relating to St. James and the route to Santiago de Compostela. I found it tawdry, and totally depressing, yet it comes probably closer to the true meanings of pilgrims than does my inflated idealism.

On the question of beauty the Cistercians and the Cluniacs differed vehemently. The Cluniacs, who lived under the vow of poverty, urged the idea on the nobility that sacrifice of their worldly goods brings spiritual benefits. Penitents who wished to ensure their salvation gave handsomely to the church, in particular to Cluny. There was a certain cachet in this too, just as there is today for arts benefactors. Whatever the inner motivation of the patrons, the order became rich and gorgeously endowed. The churches were built and adorned in such a way as to reflect the idea of the heavenly kingdom. Seeing such treasures and sanctuaries, one would just imagine what further glory was waiting for the blessed in the hereafter. For a Platonist, the argument is sound; it is still put forward today.

St. Bernard would have none of it. To know God, you must study his creation, he said. Learn from nature by living in it. The created order imitates the heavenly. This is the period when the idea that the microcosm was the replication of the macrocosm flourished, the former being the instructor for the latter. Bernard's opinion of the Cluniac way is scathing. He finds it ostentatious and distracting; people would rather look at the variety of sculpted images than study the law of God, he said. What galled him – how contemporary he sounds here! – is that "the church glitters on all sides, but the poor are destitute; her stones are covered with gilding, and her children are deprived of clothes. O vanity of vanities!" He was anti-urban, railing against the distractions and fleshpots of the city. He condemned the use of logic to study scripture, claiming it was to be known through the heart, not the reason. "You will find more in the forests than in books; trees and rocks will teach you things that no master can tell you." Paradoxically, Bernard spent much of his life consorting with kings, arguing with that advocate of the use of reason, Peter Abelard, and preaching crusades against the Moslems and the heretical Cathars. Not much forest life for him.

Sad to say, no sooner had Bernard died than the monks of Cîteaux began to swing over to the Cluniac way, and accept rich donations. Their methods of agriculture were so successful that their wealth grew. Eventually they were being called proud and ostentatious by their detractors. Many of these silent ascetics became bishops. It seems that the way of the Cistercians was either too demanding to be carried out in its fullness, or it carried within its great ideals the seed of its own diversions and distortions.

Bernard is the greatest religious figure of his century, not an easy person to love on account of his stringent demands and intractable opinions, yet full of charisma. When he entered the dispirited Cistercian order he brought thirty men with him; about forty years later there were about three hundred and fifty abbeys where there had been only a handful. Louis Mumford, tracing the historical development of the city, says that "As long as the medieval complex was intact, a constant stream of disillusioned worldly men and women turned from the marketplace and the battlefield to seek the quiet contemplative round of the monastery and the convent." This is an interesting take on the monastic vocation, to see it as a withdrawal from, not a going towards. I can see that, considering the predicament women were in, it might indeed be for them an escape from a dreadful life: but I always thought most people chose the life of a religious from positive, compelling motives. Morris says they came through a mixture of confidence and despair. I suppose it is all a matter of degree.

Here is that detachment notion again. In this situation, it means withdrawal from the attractions of the cultured world, not the natural one, where God is to be contemplated. The monks pursued detachment by denying themselves luxuries: fine clothes, food, servants, ecclesiastical adornments. I think there are two general kinds of detachment. The first type is where you withdraw from something in order to do something else. Scholarship is like that: you detach yourself from sense experience so you can think about it, a kind of delayed gratification. In the case of scholarship I wonder, though: since the gratification is in the cognitive discoveries, I suspect that experience as such is delayed forever.

The second type of detachment is where you withdraw from something and have nowhere to go. No goals, no desires. It can lead either to anomie, or to mysticism, the experience of the divine unadulterated by one's needs and ulterior motives. The question is, is whatever is left – the silence, the deprivation, the absence – empty or full? That can only be answered by those who experience this state, who describe it but don't analyse it.

My experience of such things is neither very extensive nor profound, but it has surely occurred. When I was meditating frequently, my "transcendent" experience was paramount and joyous. I cannot really describe it except as a kind of knowing that is unified, that melds thought and will and emotion into a wordless understanding. Sometimes it launches one's consciousness like an arrow into the blue, shooting outward towards an unseen goal. Mostly, though, it is like the song of a nightingale, continuous, invisible, totally engaging, excluding everything else, while disclosing everything. It is superbly convincing; it is Carlyle's Everlasting Yea.

Another sort of vision comes more readily these days. It arrives unbidden and unexpectedly. I may be listening to music, or staring at an array of exuberantly colourful flowers in a garden, or listening to a friend speak, reading a poem, walking down a street in France. Suddenly a feeling will grip me, filling my whole body, almost like an orgasm, and I want to expand my boundaries to embrace everything within sight and sound. The world is enhanced, made richer by what means I do not know; it is like what the lark's song does to the land-scape. There is that Wordsworthian "sense sublime/Of something ... deeply interfused" and once again I know I am not mistaken. The world is full of divinity, often lost through neglect or cover-up, sometimes wonderfully found.

For the first type of experience, to consider the deep metaphysical question such as death, truth, consciousness, the future, you have to be in a certain position which is almost physical. You must look at them as though face on, so that they fill your entire horizon. There is nothing outside your body, just the question itself.

If you step to one side, then you can look at the question from a certain perspective, sociological, historical, personal or philosophical. You are approaching it from one side of yourself. It is only when you give yourself up to the question again, letting it take hold and surround you that you know about the stepping aside you usually do.

People sometimes think that this absorption in the question is really only a partial approach. The understanding we arrive at defies logic, and we must never give up on logic, we think. Why not, for goodness' sake? Did logic construct the universe, give birth, encourage growth? Did it even come forward with such ideas as goodness and truth? Is the reason we strive for these a logical one? No, their base is transcendental, however much one claims it depends on practical reason. The power of and necessity for deep questions has hegemony over logic. They outclass it by infinite degrees.

Some think the absorption in deep questions is impractical, useless, a waste of time in the end, only for dreamers who like that sort of thing, not for the real world. All I can say is, once you have allowed yourself to be immersed in these questions, you know what the real world is, or could be. After that, all your practice begins to change. The questions have powerful implications. No question is entirely abstract. If I think about death, my own is included. If I search for an understanding of error, sorrow, love, I cannot avoid using my own experience as subject. The more I can bring to the question, the more I shall know it in its ultimacy. In a way this fits into the Cistercian pattern, which emphasizes self-knowledge.

There were lots of otherworldly mystics or visionaries in the late Middle Ages, many of them women. Women mystics were a growth industry. It is easy enough to speculate on the reasons for this from psychological and sociological points of view: women were disenfranchised and powerless, and the times were out of joint. Biblical scholar Gerda Lerner says they needed authorization, since they were denied the priesthood and other public roles. I am inclined to think that, given a capacity for love, thought and desire that was hardly drawn upon in their circumscribed lives, women had more room in their souls for the mind of God to make itself clear. Religious experience always goes beyond the boundaries, intellectual and ethical, of the religious structure; it must, or else the whole thing, church and people, becomes moribund. My spiritual reach is always exceeding my grasp and I am not alone.

Where I fit in between these two ideal types is a lot closer to the Cluniac than the Cistercian way. When I read St. Bernard's attack on the Clunaics I winced: it was getting too close. He said that the monks of Cluny loved the good life, sometimes eating so well that they burst with indigestion. Ah, that olive oil, goat's cheese and Côtes du Rhone! I do have my moments of asceticism, but they are just that, moments. And the retreat from the world, well, that is coming to Campagnac, which hardly qualifies as the desert of sensory deprivation. Its debt to the Cistercian ideal lies in the fact that it is a place where inwardness matters, where consciousness of the natural world is always present, where the busyness of the everyday intrudes only slightly, and where much of the effort to produce this joyous retreat house has been ours. I was delighted to discover that Thomas Merton, perhaps the most famous Cistercian of them all now, lived as a boy in Saint-Antonin, the nearby town where we go to Sunday market. To get there from the train station in another town, he could have passed through our village; that must account for its Cistercian twinges. More wonderful still is the discovery that Merton was powerfully affected by the atmosphere of this whole region, so much so that he could write some 30 years later: "It is... of great importance to me that I have known the narrow streets of Cordes.... It is important to me that I have walked the dusty road under the plane trees from St. Antonin to Caylus and from Caylus to Puylagarde.... It is important for me to have stood in the ruined castles of Penne and Najac...to have smelled the sun and the dust in the streets of Toulouse or Narbonne. There are times when I am mortally homesick for the South of France, where I was born."

Leaving Flaran, this graceful yet hollow place, like a cicada shell after the beetle has gone, I wonder: maybe the fact that the stones say so little is evidence of their Cistercian character, so materially unimportant that even the fabric of old lives is a thin, imperceptible veil. A real emptiness.

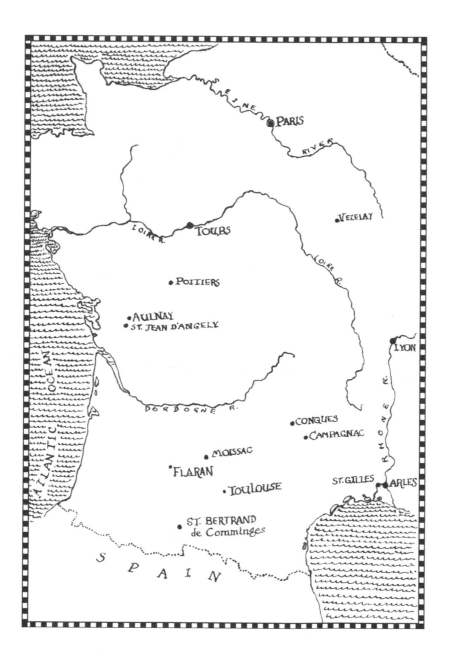

urquhart 1919

CHAPTER 6

— SAINT-JEAN D'ANGÉLY, MOISSAC —

John. *Known as the Baptist. Saint. b. probably* AD *1, Palestine. d. Jerusalem. Ascetic, desert-dwelling preacher and latter-day prophet. Recognizes Jesus as the anticipated Messiah, baptizes him in Jordan river. Beheaded by Herod at the request of his stepdaughter Salome.*

Peter. *Saint.*

The architectural legacy of the great Benedictine order of Cluny is slight. Very few noted buildings survive intact. Vézelay would have fallen down had it not been for Viollet-le-Duc's restorative work. The great motherhouse at Cluny, at one time the largest religious structure in the West, has been reduced to a few fragments, a victim of Revolutionary anticlericalism, state indifference and callous looting.

In Saint-Jean d'Angély, not far from Aulnay, where there was once a landmark church, I find a strange assemblage of buildings, or what's left of them. Two towers, the conventual buildings, plus part of a rib and buttress, are all that is left of the constructions belonging to this abbey, begun in the ninth century, destroyed, rebuilt, destroyed, and partially rebuilt. The Gothic buttressed section now forms part of a later church. The rest is well-kept ruins.

I came here because I was intrigued by its original claim to importance. At the time of high pilgrimage the church boasted one of two said-to-be-authentic heads of John the Baptist, the other being several days' walk away at Amiens in the north. I haven't read that there was any dispute over which one was genuine, and which belonged to an impostor or a misnamed saint. The distance is probably one reason why people were able to accept the existence of both. Another reason may be that the Saint-Jean head seems to have disappeared about 860, when travel was interrupted by the chaotic post-Charlemagne period of wars and skirmishes, and was conveniently found in its hiding place in 1010, when folk did longen to goon on pilgrimage.

These explanations don't really help me to understand the strange medieval logic. Can one saint have two heads, perhaps? We know that identical miracle stories can be told of any number of saints. People believed they were exempla: the more often the story was told, the more effective the miracle and its worker were thought to be. So if a saint could cure three women of a cataract in the left eye even though they lived in three neighbouring towns, for instance, why couldn't St. John have two heads with which to support the faithful in two different towns? Did he need a head, actually, in the phase of life in which he was situated? Would he need it before the final resurrection, when all bodies would be raised whole? If physicality was no problem, then he could send his head where he liked.

This is my weird attempt at medieval reasoning. Although it matters to me to try to understand this mind-set, it didn't matter very much to the pilgrims. I thought in my ignorance that the head of St. John would have required a vast church to hold all the devout, and I expected a sizeable town based on tourism. Apparently this was never so. Gurevich says that, while the church fathers regarded St. John as first among saints (Aymeri Picaud de Parthenay-le-Vieux, the supposed author of the twelfth-century *Guide du Pèlerin*, says a choir of one hundred monks venerated the relic night and day) popular belief did not. People judged saints according to their miracle-working capacities, and John had not produced any. So let the other town keep its head, much good may it do them. At least Saint-Jean d'Angély was a stop on the route to Santiago de Compostela.

Relics were often used for fund-raising, says John James, sent around to the neighbouring towns to collect money for the abbeys. I noticed that the abbey at Saint-Jean, which had to be reconstructed after the Vikings destroyed an earlier one, wasn't dedicated until 1050, some forty years after the Baptist's head was discovered. I guess that proves it: lack of miracles slows up donations a whole lot, even though the kings of France and of Navarre gave of their best. It also points out, to me at least, the irony of a very rich religious establishment soliciting donations in order to honour a saint who wore sackcloth and ate locusts and wild honey.

Standing sentinels to nothing in particular, the elaborate towers dominate a broad, open green space behind them, in which a group of young people are rehearsing a piece of medieval polyphony in a contemporary tonality that owes nothing to its antecedents, in preparation for a theatrical performance that evening. Although the idea of a presentation in that setting is intriguing, we decide to give it a miss. These are summer students taking a workshop at the royal abbey alongside the ruins, a trim eighteenth-century building which is now a music school.

Some historians think that the *chansons de geste*, those heroic and romantic tales told by the troubadours, were passed along via the pilgrimage routes. This is Aquitaine after all, where Eleanor's mysterious daughter Marie de France held court, encouraging the art of courtly love with all its attendant cultural ways. Recently I came across a joyous recording of twelfth-century love songs written by women troubadours, called *trobairitz*. These poet-musicians, of whom a very few are known by name today, sang for the important nobility of the region. One of the poets is the Condesa de Dia, wife of Guillaume II of Poitiers; another is the wife of the Count of Provence, who was Alfonso II of Spain. The connections between Spain, Languedoc and Provence are clear. What better way to pass these songs along than via the popular pilgrimage routes, and what better way to relieve the harshness of the way than by listening to stories of noble women eager to cuckold their abominable husbands and lie with their worthy and passionate lovers. I wonder what the music repertoire includes for these young summer students here.

In 1989, the Centre for European Culture "Saint Jacques de Compostelle" was established here. It holds two-week seminars during the school year for young people fifteen to eighteen years old. Classes of students come from three different countries for each session; the aim is to give them a sense of the European history and culture that they have in common. The program of study focuses appropriately on the Middle Ages.

In the abbey building there is an exhibition on the silent language of medieval religious imagery, with photographs of carving and frescoes. It is an excellent primer of bodyspeak. I learn that hands and feet tell all: hands resting on the chin = dolour; on another's shoulder = love; hands crossed = powerlessness; a finger pointed upwards = teaching with authority; fingers laced in front = powerlessness; feet crossed = power, as does sitting in the frontal position; counting on one's fingers = teaching; clasping another's wrist = control; one hand on one's chin, the other on one's elbow = extreme sorrow. Here is a partial set of clues for interpreting those narratives designed for the illiterate and the lately come.

As a town, Saint-Jean d'Angély does not bowl you over, but it is good to know it is there, doing its best to keep the important parts of its history alive.

All the churches I have deliberately chosen to visit have now, or have had, a relic or two of saints, many names unknown to me, usually French, and probably for the most part local people, whose reputation was earned right near the spot where I have been standing. I chose these places from among the hundreds of possibilities because I hoped that they, being the most famous, would still be somewhat intact. I did not reckon on the Wars of Religion, and those doughty Huguenot avengers, nor later on, with the Revolution, although most of the architectural damage and relic-snatching was over by then.

That was the overt reason I chose them. Since I have been poking about, though, I am beginning to suspect another one, and, as is my wont, I will rush in to concoct a theory that is not even warm, let alone half-baked. My own motives are suspect: if it were really just architectural marvels I was after, why would I be so caught up in the sole remaining fragment of the crypt that (it was said) might (at one time) have held the (whole or part) body of Roland (are we even sure about him)? I'm no relic hunter in the old sense, but still.... What is this "still"?

Medieval people could not overdose on relics. They gathered up all they could get their hands on, by trade, gift, theft, division, and brought them home. They even placed their bets on noble people who were not canonized yet. After the battle of Roncevaux, in which Roland and all his faithful warriors died defending faith and country against the Saracens or the wild Basques, depending on whom you read, Charlemagne had the bodies of the soldiers distributed to different parish churches in Gascony, presumably in the hope that some would be efficacious. Louis XI overwhelmed the church of the Holy Innocents in Paris by presenting them with "a whole Innocent" in a crystal shrine. *Quelle largesse.*

As with many legitimate businesses, there is a black market: some people thrived on, would you believe it, faking relics! The eleventh-century monk Raoul Glaber describes a man he came across who was digging up the bones of quite ordinary men, putting them in caskets and selling them as relics. On one occasion an entire church was built to contain these unwarranted bones, but the night after the church was consecrated, monks praying there saw black apparitions rise out of the reliquaries and leave the church.

From one point of view, admittedly a twentieth-century one that could not have been shared by most medieval people, relics were good business, their dispersal a brilliant marketing plan. The Cluniac monks were the chief distributors, making sure that the abbey churches under their care especially along the pilgrimage routes were well supplied, even if it meant dismembering the saint so there would be enough to go around. It worked well: Abbot Suger, whose glorious achievement is the royal pantheon and treasure house of Saint-Denis, described the crowds who lined up to kiss the relics in the basilica as so vast that the women were almost trampled upon. In addition, the making of precious reliquaries was a bourgeoning source of income for gold-smiths, while other craftspeople thrived on the sale of miniatures of shrines, reliquaries, and special vials to hold water or oil dispensed by the monks at the saints' *domaines*.

It is unlikely that even those who were making money from the relic routes would have had this crass, single-minded attitude to what they were doing. Certainly those who came for the relics did not. Theirs was a composite view of what the saints were like, and what they were doing in this world and the next. A good saint, one you could put your trust in, was, says Gurevich, "a nimbus-crowned magi-cian filled with goodness and compassion." Saints were expected to do miraculous things, or at least to bring about desired natural occur-rences that were not taking place by any other means. If they did not do this, they were abandoned; like film stars, their brightness depended on the magic they conveyed.

Even if these holy, learned and charitable people did not produce any wonders before they died, there was still time afterwards, and that is of course where the relics came in. In this popular view, time had no real break, the saint continued to work for the people, who continued to importune her/him to do something to help them. That they were not overawed by the presence among them of such a wonder worker can be seen from the way they spoke: "What have you done, Benedict, are you some kind of lazybones? Do you sleep all the time? How could you permit this to happen to your servant?" all the while holding the relics and banging on the altar. Apparently the saints did not get angry, they just woke up and did what was required.

Gurevich, whose book has made me appreciate more than anything else the complexity of religious belief in the Middle Ages, distinguishes between magic and religion in this way: in a magical view, human beings are one with the natural world, and magical rites are simply part of the process of making things happen as they should. Conversely, the Christian religious view separates and alienates the human from the natural by anthropomorphizing the divine. Medieval people did not distinguish one view from the other, but operated on both fronts at once. The church intelligentsia did. They thought the real difference lay in who performed the supranatural miracles, not necessarily in the acts themselves. Saints, shamans and soothsayers were on different sides of the bed. The church fathers did anathematize a few tricks of the magician's trade, objects that no saint would ever use, such as potions and anything that contained a mouse. Sending naked young girls out into the fields to bring on rain, or to assure a good harvest, was definitely not in the ritual guidelines for saints. (The rites took place nevertheless.) Many other performances, however, which we might call magical, the church did not. The common people and the illiterate seem to have amassed all these ideas without discrimination or concern and ignored the clergy's warnings against paganism.

It amazes me that, at least two hundred years after the barbarians had left France, and eight hundred after Christianity came officially to the country, clerics were having difficulty getting their exclusive message across, even with fifty thousand new churches, and all those relics. Nothing changes.

Feminist theologians are struggling to find new ways of describing the divine, ultimate reality, the ground of being, etc. Certainly these terms will not do; Western worshipping minds abhor the vacuum that is complete abstraction. The biblical, semi-abstract idea that God is spirit (really breath, but that went the way of the fathers long ago) works well with a three-stage universe, and a power in control in whose image and under whose authority we too control the natural world. Feminists are working with a different geography, more like the magical medieval view, emphasizing this natural world as the first, perhaps the only, area of activity. In their need to give divinity an image, some have returned to the pre-Christian one of Gaia, the earth. Taking this concrete direction has led some feminists away from Christianity, but the idea should not be dismissed altogether.

The important gift that all these thinkers have given us, both the medieval folk and the feminist intelligentsia, is that of a re-evaluation of the natural world and our way of being in it. The world itself will show us divinity, if we but set out to absorb it, through all the perceptual and cognitive means available to us.

There is a startlingly relevant saying of Jesus: to those who have ,more will be given, and to those who have not, even the little they have will be taken away. While Protestants and capitalists may agree readily, I think there is a rare and more marvellous logic to this statement when it applies to relics. According to contemporary pilgrim/writer Michel Gardère, Joan of Arc is said to have fought the English with the sword used by Charles Martel to halt the Arabs. Never mind the time gap of about seven hundred years. I think the point is Joan ought to have used that sword since it was obviously a winner. How she got it is of no consequence: it should be hers; she deserved it.

Then there is Roland's sword Durandel, whose pommel contained one of St. Peter's teeth, some of St. Basil's blood, hairs from the head of St. Denis, and a fragment of the clothing worn by the Blessed Virgin. It was a holy sword used in a holy cause, driving out infidels. Of course it would come mightily empowered: the need was great, and the sword bearer was noble. Ask not how Roland got these holy relics, though I suppose all good things came to Charlemagne and his knights, those Christian worthies whose exploits became legendary.

A theory of semantic depletion states that those objects, places or and rituals that no longer hold religious significance become treated as art forms. One of the adjectives people use to describe their heightened experiences these days is "magical": it was a magical place or occasion, meaning I think that it is beautiful, joyful, marvellous. I wonder if here is the germ of the reversal of this theory – semantic revival, maybe – in which a world divested of the sense of the sacred through many centuries of rationalizing thought begins to regain its holiness little by little. A contemporary Italian architect said, "We are killing the moonlight." Perhaps through pilgrimages, tracking down relics, ruins and the like, finding the old pre-Christian sacrality, we will revive it. Old hierophanies guard their sacredness. They have an afterlife. They glow in the dark.

Although there is only a drawing extant to indicate the grandeur of the motherhouse of Cluny, one of the order's finest constructions is with us still, in part, and in restored form. It sits in Moissac, an hour or so away from Campagnac. It is a small, insignificant town, no bigger today than it was in the Middle Ages. There's nowhere special to eat or to wander; the river's banks are for commerce, not for *flânerie*. (I love that word: it means strolling or idling, and seems to express it better than the English.) There is really only one drawing card, and that is the doorway and cloister of the church of Saint Peter. You don't need any greater reason to visit: these are astonishing.

The great abbey buildings have dwindled down to the church and a couple of other derelicts because both town and monastic establishment have had the now familiar, miserable history of sacking, pillaging, fire and peacetime neglect. Even in the mid-nineteenth century the engineers putting a rail line through the town wanted to demolish the cloister to make room for it; a public outcry and the help of Viollet-le-Duc saved it. The admiration for Romanesque had gone into a long decline by this time, not to reappear until this century. The church, the latest of several built on this spot, is a conglomerate of a lot of rather ordinary ideas with the exception of the twelfth-century bits. This pattern parallels the abbey's own history. It had one really brilliant reign, from the mid-eleventh to mid-twelfth centuries, after which it got sacked again, and then hit by the Wars of Religion.

The reason for its success was its adoption by Cluny as one of the order's major abbeys. They wanted it for a particular job: to organize the Spanish section of the route to Santiago de Compostela. Moissac became second in importance to the motherhouse, building and supervising priories and hostels along the way. It is interesting that the monks were so active in the mission field, so to speak, when their Rule was quite specific that prayer and praise were the royal road to heaven.

How well this cloister would have suited the meditative pattern of Cluniac life, with its wide stone pavements and broad greensward in the centre where there was once a fountain. The four galleries have single and twinned columns, each supporting a capital carved on all four sides. One could, I suppose, make one prayerful circuit on the cloister side, another on the garden side, and two others going clockwise and counter-clockwise to look at the other two faces, and each time you would have learned something different. With seventy-six capitals each with four sides, there was a lot to learn.

Most of the capitals are what is called historiated, with fragments of stories from the Bible and the lives of the saints. Some are inhabited (sounds like a birdhouse on a pole), showing unspecific humans and animals. Some are decorative with a kind of floral fecundity that comes right from the imagination. Some of the stories are told in several scenes and others get just one vignette. It is amazing how a sculptor could achieve such depth of meaning in such a small surface which is, in effect, an inverted pyramid that slopes up and towards you. One of my favourite carvings is the miracle of the fish, where with a few curling and waving lines a deep boat set on a very tiny sea can be shown to have just landed a wonderfully disproportionate catch.

I found myself wondering why certain important themes were not there – the Birth of Jesus, the Last Supper, the Passion and the Crucifixion – when just about everything else you can think of is. It made me realize how little is known about these stones, and how much more I would like to know. Who did the carving? Were they local people or itinerant masons? How long did it take them? Was this the work of just one person? Who designed the program for the cloister, leaving out the twelve disciples at that Last Supper table, but including Jesus washing their feet which took place minutes before? Would the designs have come from the monks in charge, or from the sculptors? How much leeway did the carvers have? Did they get their ideas from other buildings and sculptors, and how many were their own?

Did anyone write about these superb carvings as they were being created? the monks? travellers? pilgrims? Why isn't there an archive telling who the sculptors were, how long they took, and how much they were paid, assuming that money did change hands? In a few places, like Vézelay and Saint-Sernin, we know the name of the sculptor, but mainly they were anonymous. It is not because the individual was not yet distinguished socially from the group (we learn the names of the abbots) but that the artist wasn't important enough to matter.

In the centre of the cloister six pilgrims were sitting down laughing and getting acquainted, one couple and a foursome. They were there for the whole two hours we were, and spent probably five or ten minutes looking at the sculptures, and no more in the church. This stop is for relaxation and camaraderie, not architecture and symbol.

They did have a good look at the doorway, though. It would be almost sacrilege to miss it. Here is a tympanum as grand as the one at Vézelay and at Conques, with the extra strength of scenes in relief on each side of the door, and the marvellously sinuous figures of four great prophets and apostles, Isaiah, Jeremiah, Paul and Peter, draped along the door and the *trumeau*. It is not the entire cast of the Bible in stone, but a good deal of it.

Sculptors who work on a tympanum seem to be able to use the space to bring a dynamism to their theme that is often missing in other forms. I am thinking about the thrilling moment in the Vézelay scene, where Jesus sends the disciples out to win people's hearts; the tenderness of the Nativity at Saint-Bertrand-de-Comminges; and the chilling effect of being damned at Conques. Here, for all that it is the crucial moment – it is just about the end of time as we know it – the mood is remarkably serene and relaxed. That is because we have not quite got to the Last Judgment; art historian Calkins says it is the moment before. The devils may be assembling in the background, but here in Moissac we see only those who are happily prepared for the apocalypse: the angels, the symbols of the four Evangelists, and the most enchanting group of twenty-four old men you could ever imagine. These are the elders of St. John the Divine's vision, sitting in rows, each holding a harp and a vial containing the prayers of the saints. Most of them are looking up at Christ in glory, with interest and attention, as if he might be going to say something important. They could be at a football game, their postures are so casual: feet crossed or spread apart, sitting sideways with heads tilted back in different positions, holding their little harps as though they were programs or closed umbrellas, the vials held like everyday jars or bags of peanuts. These are handsome, warmly human people, whom you would like to know, and perhaps you will if you end up on the right side when the time comes.

On the bas-reliefs on each side of this vast door, two lifestyle choices are made perfectly clear: goodies on the right, baddies on the left. While the infancy narrative of Jesus is charmingly told in several scenes, as usual it is the grisly pictures that catch one's attention. Here they are so worn away that they seem worse than they might have been originally. At the bottom of this truly base collection is a person-sized relief that is supposed to represent unchastity. Of course it is a woman, with two serpents sucking at her breasts and a frog going at her genitals. Facing her is a devil with distended stomach and another frog emerging from his mouth. Apparently the virtue of chastity, or its opposite, was never applied to men, even though monks vowed to be chaste and often were not.

I suppose it was that last image that got me thinking about power. I had to come to it sooner or later, and just before the Last Judgment is as good a place as any. The more I read the history of the church and its adversaries, the more I dislike power. What is common to all the vagaries of the Middle Ages (and every other time) is how life is structured to give one group control over everyone else's lives. Land was the currency, the traded material, status, the value, but power was the game. I don't know whether people got their jollies from "lording it over" others, or whether they simply did not see them as people. Most likely status beliefs were so realistic to them that they "knew" others didn't have rights.

If you were a peasant you would naturally think the same way. Both you and the lord you served knew the rules and kept to them for the most part; this was how God had set up the world, this was how things were. Of course there was deviant thinking – those heretical, anti-establishment Cathars had plenty of supporters among the herdsmen – and lots of unbelievers or half-believers. The sense of reality that they all lived by was probably shared, though.

For the nobles and kings the structure of reality and the rules that supported it were the same as those for the peasants, but in the power game played at the lordly level there were other rules that caused the positions to change. The rules had to do with fighting (stealing land), making treaties (trading land), and making marriages (acquiring more land).

The church was in this game too, although the means of acquiring land were different. Its main purpose, however, was to keep ultimate control of people's lives, making sure that it, and not the kings, had the final say. At the time I am chiefly interested in, things were not going too well for the church. The Eastern branch had split off from the West, setting up its own parallel sphere of influence. The kingdoms and duchies of what is now France had been weakened and impoverished by many invasions, giving the church little material from which to draw. From the point of view of both church and state something had to be changed for the better.

One of the best means of restoring religious and national pride was the Crusades. Their aim was to pull the country together through a holy cause, and also to send powerful knights out of the country for a long while, giving kings time to gather strength against them. The church's second thrust was to re-establish other pilgrimage routes, primarily the one to Santiago de Compostela now that Spain had been recovered from the Saracens. Finally there was the anti-heresy crusade against the Cathars, and the beginning of the Inquisition. Through all these ventures the church acquired prestige, land and power. Monasteries got rich: those of the fighting monks – the Templars; the travel agency monks – the Benedictines of Cluny; the architect/collector monks (Cluny again); and the heresy hunters – the Dominicans. They collected land from the conquered, the heretics and the grateful. It was a golden age.

Acquiring power is one thing; keeping control is another. In this period the church had, I think, the biggest handful of means for social control it has ever had. Besides the money and land it acquired from these new ventures, there were alliances with kings, which always meant exchanges of goods, material for spiritual. Within its own ecclesiastical sphere there was first and foremost the theology of heaven and hell, especially hell. There was the classification of and emphasis upon sin: confession was public, which helped keep matters fresh and jangling. There were the punishments; the commonest of these was penance, one of which was to be sent on pilgrimage. The worst punishment was excommunication, which had heavy penance attached to it. At the end of this there was forgiveness, where the sinner was brought back again into the theological frame of heaven and hell.

There were means of prepaying one's way, so that hell was avoided: the cleansing ground for sin called purgatory, and the system of intercessory prayer. For some there was no choice at all: unconfessed heretics, and particularly Jews, who were so hated that they were driven from Spain to France, and later from France to any place that would take them. Other pagans were treated as pariahs, but none with the vehemence shown towards Jews, for whom hell on earth and/or afterwards were the only options.

In spite of all these forceful attempts to control minds and lives, and even with the rampant belief that the end of the world was at hand, people were still not entirely convinced, devoted or even chastened. Behind the church's back they still believed in fairies, spooks and old-time deities. They still had fun, too – didn't spend all their time shaking in their shoes at the retribution to come.

If I were a hard-line feminist (my gender right or wrong) I would say that the church's bloody-minded ways of grasping and maintaining power came about because men were in charge. But there is no cause to say that. What I will say is this: these things happened *and* men were in charge. I cannot say that it would have been any different had women had the power. When power comes into it the sexes have a strange habit of performing alike. Look at all the divisions in the women's movement. In some sections my vote wouldn't count since I am not a lesbian. (This is like the old ideological purity games played between monks and the secular orders, for instance.) Other feminist forums will take me in even if I am married, have children, have a job, and love to cook. Round and round we go.

Jesus' great contribution to this mortal combat for the soul was to pooh-pooh it, and place the emphasis on a personal, spiritual relationship, his and ours, with the divine. No matter how different ages have chosen to rationalize and take away parts of his speech and behaviour that didn't suit them, when you look at Jesus squarely, he stood for individualism, communal groups, rejection of power as a means to an end or as an end in itself. He was subversive, hating the self-serving conservatism of the power élite of the synagogue. (He dismisses Rome; it's not part of his mission.) Being no sociologist, he didn't know about the routinization of charisma: that, having passed the torch to Peter and the others, we would eventually end up with a structure that is, to put a kind face on it, no better than it should be.

Jesus was a man with soaring ambition and not a dime to his name. (That is not mentioned actually in scripture, but he certainly lived like a friar.) Had he been a woman, he would have had a lot more trouble getting a following in his society. Ultimately his gender does not affect his message or his goals, but the old question "What price power?" has to be asked and answered by men and women over and over again. It will not go away.

Why am I still involved, to the slight degree that I am? I don't know. Because the church is beautiful. Because it is better than its power structure. Because there is nothing else to compare with it. Because it has some fine people. Because it has some keen new theological thinking. Because I hope it will change. Because I hope it will change me too.

Clearly my feelings are ambivalent. I am quick to condemn the church's use of power in the past, and the vestiges of that mind-set in the present. Yet I love the heritage it has left us, in sacred spaces, liturgy, music, and its ideals, if not often its practice. I am coming to love its saints and to see in them some vague hope for a new vision.

I wonder if my questions and my attack are misplaced. I keep asking, how do I avoid falling into the sexist autocracy trap, when everything about the structure, even the superb Psalms, keeps pulling me back in? Perhaps in putting the wrong questions first, I am hiding the important questions, so I will not have to deal with them: a child's technique, where you refuse to answer the crucial question posed to you by asking another instead.

To the mainstream orthodox, it will sound scandalous if I speculate that the question of the church's role today does not matter. It will sort itself out. The church may not in the end be the central focus of Christianity, my own and that of many others. It is after all a political and social structure. Jesus' church, which he told Peter he would form, may be quite different.

The church question for me has always stood as a first barricade against the new life in Christ. Now that I am trying to see beyond it, I must ask instead, how does God include the feminine, and how does this inclusion fit in with biblical narrative and theology? I count on the legacy of the church, these stones, these saints, to help me out.

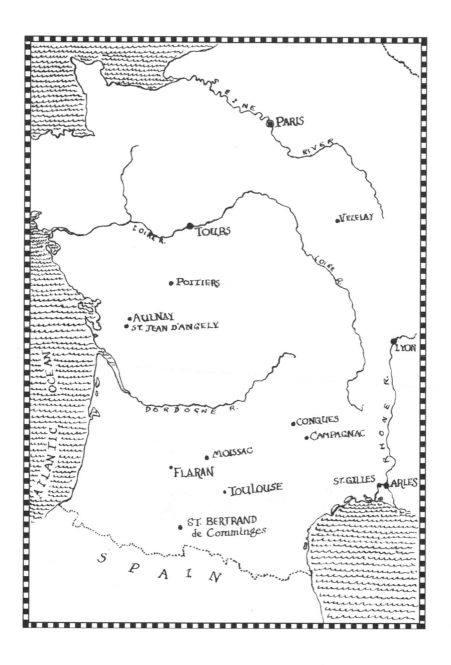

nave - St. Sernin. Toulouse.
elevation + MPI.

CHAPTER 7

— TOULOUSE —

Saturnin or **Sernin**. *Saint and martyr. b?, d. 250, Toulouse. A Gaul, converted to Christianity. As he refused to perform the rites of ancestral worship in the temple, he was tied to a bull destined for sacrifice which dragged him through the city. Buried surreptitiously by fearful Christians. Later St. Hilaire raised a monument over the tomb. Bones removed to new basilica in the fifth century. Pilgrimages began.*

Minerva. *Goddess. Origin Etruscan, adopted by Romans. Formed triad with Jupiter and Juno. Patron of wisdom, arts and letters, music. Protector of schools, commerce and industry. Festival took place during the spring equinox. Particularly honoured by artisans, flutists, doctors.*

Polyglot, schizophrenic, southern belle: that's Toulouse. To some she is partly hideous, growing beyond her means, impossible to navigate, and of middling interest. To others she is a beacon of urban culture in an otherwise somnolent countryside. For all those reasons and some others I find her fascinating, the part that is not hideous having decided to go its own way, not copying tediously the urban mind-set of all the other large French cities.

As I wander around the core of the city it seems that throughout its history, every marauding or style-setting newcomer has had something to add in brick or stone, and plenty of samples still remain. What evidence of town planning there is appears in little clusters here and there with nothing too dauntingly regular. There are the natural barriers for the pedestrian in the form of a river and the canal, and two planned boulevards that circle much of the city and prevent you from becoming totally lost. At the same time, I can guarantee that if you take what purports to be a straight street leading directly to some desired goal, you will overshoot the mark and end up in a totally unexpected and probably intriguing place. Much of the city is dilapidated, in need of heavy repair; much of it is just fading away, but that part was never handsome in the first place. Having said that, I find most of it, both shabby and select, just a delight. With the opposite opinion, Valérie Hubault from Campagnac, who has lived in Toulouse for six years, can hardly wait to get out to the suburbs. She is twenty-five, and lives in a quarter full of university students and hookers. She can't bear the chaotic lodgings and the music these young people inflict upon her more mature ears.

Toulouse is my city, my alter ego. If I could draw a map of my life it would look like Toulouse: all sorts of curving, endless streets that turn back on themselves; some prosperous-looking ones that are dead ends; some grand boulevards that take high jumps over water; and small squares to rest in. It is hard to keep your focus firmly on whatever it is you came for as the city seems to be host to every age, taste and pleasure.

Apart from such analogous fantasizing, there are two main attributes of this complex city that pertain directly to my life: music and heresy. On this particular day I have decided to come to town alone on the train, avoiding all bookstores, markets and antique shops. I am going to the basilica of Saint-Sernin, the city's pride and joy, one of the numerous buildings consecrated by the pope in 1096.

It is in the university quarter where there are more students coming and going than tourists. Here is the ubiquitous man-with-dog-and-guitar combo on the front steps. Unfortunately for him the doors are closed for lunch so he will have a two-hour wait for handouts. Perhaps he is not here for that. On Sundays, with the typical Tolosan capacity for happily mixing without matching, activities around the basilica include a flea market for furnishings, old books and art. Once I was amused to see a nun claiming the main steps for her display of holy hardware, a proprietary right, I suppose.

Although I have been here often, this time I am forcing myself to take it very slowly, considering the building, if not brick by brick, then certainly segment by segment. So I sit at a café facing the east end of the basilica, coffee in one hand, drawing pencil in the other. Its five-tiered spire looks so much like a wedding cake, I cannot help thinking what a poor, uncertain day for a wedding this would be. It is a day when you would worry if it would rain, if the wind would abate, whether the canopies would be any protection at all. The air is heavy, the sky a cover of tin, the wind cool but no consolation. It is the worst possible day to see this lovely building, and yet its presence does not change. It is just the same in sun and cloud. There is no moral here; it is just what the brick is like.

I have had an ongoing difference of opinion with Bob about the local brick, whose soft, dusty pink tone gives the city its name of *"la ville rose."* Looked at from a distance they seem to be slim, long bricks, giving the impression of lightness and grace. Bob says the bricks are just the same shape as ours at home, only the mortar is thicker. Today I decide to find out, and this time my engineer husband is wrong. On a part of a wall that is being repaired I measured a whole brick: it is 30 centimetres long, 15 wide, and 6 high. For once the *oeil* was not *tromped*.

Saint-Sernin's apse is like a fabric, a finely woven background covered with couching stitches, the doubled arches of the windows forming the pattern. Below the windows the pattern changes, as for a border, simpler but still interesting. There are many more details, in brick and stone, but so well integrated the effect is not busy. Durliat, one of the experts on this building, says these are very old ideas, Roman and Merovingian. Still musing on weddings, I think the pattern would make a superb dress for someone of quality though not proud, or for an actress perhaps, someone with the rare, effervescent poise of an Emma Thompson, or the grace of a Charlotte Rampling.

The basilica is not here to talk about weddings. It is here to commemorate a man who for his refusal to apostatize was torn to death by a bull. The horror of that crime could never be compensated for in the look of a building. In fact, I find traces of the saint neither here nor in the fabric of the city. Instead Saint-Sernin almost seems to be offering the other cheek, displaying grace, serenity and stability.

Viollet-le-Duc, the architect who restored Vézelay, took charge of Saint-Sernin too, making great changes to the earlier building. Now that it needs conserving work done again, after much debate it has been decided to restore it to the form it had before he muddled it up. The arch they're working on now looks so new!

The interior is a fine, handsome place even though from a purely visual point of view the long, narrow nave seems too enclosing, out of proportion. Nevertheless as a way of giving a worshipping group a sense of cohesiveness, it couldn't be better. If you want to escape and wander as you please, there are the unusual double side aisles, the same design as at Santiago de Compostela itself. The loveliness of the place has to do with its lightness and, just like the outside, with the subtle interest of the design which never intrudes on the form. Pillars of alternating stone and brick leading to brick arches, light coming in from below and above and what seems like a very high ceiling: all very uplifting, so to say.

Since I first came here fifteen years ago, the unwelcoming dingy sanctuary has been totally altered. What was a dirty gilt baldachin, the wooden canopy above the altar, has been cleaned and re-gilded and sits glowingly below the dome whose faded fresco is being restored. You have to pay to go into the spacious ambulatory, to see the recently repainted seventeenth-century figures in their brightly coloured finery, and to go down into the crypt where the relics are kept. It gives you a powerful feeling, a kind of déjà vu, of having been there in line with other pilgrims, of walking history.

While this is the part the parish seems most proud of (they call it the "tour of the holy bodies"), what I love most is the sense of the whole, especially from the outside, into which the work of several stone sculptors fits so well. The biblical scenes on the marvellous doors called the *Porte Miégeville* are carved by a master whose fine marble reliefs appear inside too. There are capitals with designs, animal and vegetable, placed very high up in the nave. Saint-Sernin, like any house, has a public face, which makes a very important statement; inside there are all the quirks, curiosities and beauties of family life.

Saint-Sernin's organ is famous, one of the great instruments of Europe. There is nothing like the sound of a fine French organ played in such a building. It is a mixture of the grandly processional and the hurdy-gurdy. It doesn't make you want to get into the parade, but rather sit back in your seat with your mouth open in wonderment. I prefer them to English organs, which may have more subtlety but miss out on this human colouring with the slight hint of fun.

I had heard recordings of this organ played by superb performers, and I was looking forward keenly to hearing the real thing. The first time I heard it was at Easter one year. On this most important day of the church year, one can expect to hear some of the greatest compositions performed. The church was packed to the doors, people standing on the steps inside. The organ did not come in until the very end of the mass. Before that, a young priest led us in hymns, which if they suited anything belonged with guitars, not an organ. Finally, as the service was over and people were getting up to leave, the organ gave out its magnificent voice. I had hoped for Bach, César Franck, or Dupré perhaps. Instead we got a galloping instrumental rendition of the Hallelujah Chorus, so hilariously inappropriate it made our day.

This year, 1996, which just happens to be the nine-hundredth anniversary of the basilica, the church is celebrating by refurbishing the organ. As far as I could discern from the information given out, it didn't need a lot of work, just cleaning and a few replacements. In conjunction with this facelift, Toulouse is having its first international organ festival. Spread over two weeks and an extra weekend are twenty-one concerts in eleven locations, for Toulouse is well endowed with fine organs. I have just happened to arrive in time for one of these events.

This time the church is packed again, but with another sort of crowd. Instead of the faithful laity, these are organ devotees, who, being a rare and complex breed, may also be Christians. What distinguishes them from my Easter companions is that they are all so keen. There is the young man in front of us with very sophisticated recording equipment, and individuals spread here and there with scores on their laps. I love the old man, perhaps seventy-five, with a silky white fringe around his otherwise bald head, wearing loose-fitting black, ambling in at the last minute, his scores under his arm. I think there is a music scholar like him at every serious concert I have attended. As he reaches the front, where someone has kept a seat for him, rows of smiles surround him. A good teacher, perhaps. In the interval, threesomes and foursomes, who look like students, are intently conversing, perhaps analyzing the recitalist's performance. This totally focused, heightened seriousness is missing in many assemblies of Christians in the churches I know; there they look, for the most part, proper, self-congratulatory or bored.

For these virtuosi performances, the festival has erected a giant projection screen in front of the altar so we can see the organist at work. It makes the church look like a concert hall, quite secularized. I find it disturbing, as I cannot keep my eyes off the screen, which shows a pair of hands moving from one manual to another – not unexpected, that – and two assistants reaching forward to pull stops for the player. It does nothing to enhance the performance itself. Whoever came up with this idea has put the emphasis in the wrong place. I suppose TV is responsible for this switching about, where you can watch a flamboyant performer (Diane Bish comes immediately to mind) playing marvellous music that is diminished and flattened by television's inadequate speakers. The trade-off isn't worth it.

The reason the organ is called the king of instruments probably stems from the fact that it and no other can fill a huge space completely. When it is at its fullest range of colour and volume, even with the distracting screen, it conquers the body and soul together. It lifts me out of myself and takes me...nowhere, because it stops me thinking about a place, a goal, an association with something else. I am wholly absorbed in sound, ecstatic.

The three chorales of César Franck are like that, some of the time, although the organist frequently changes the colours of the music in ways that make no musical sense to me. It is almost as though he is doing an introduction to the multitudes of combinations of sounds one can produce on a grand organ with so many stops. Then another organist plays a Widor symphony, not the famous wedding music one, but the "Romane," which is dedicated to Saint-Sernin. It is so smooth-ly presented that it seems to be coming from an entirely different instrument. The performance points to the composition alone – not to itself, not to the instrument, to the what, not the how. This is not a great work, but a handsome one, with superb moments. People who have never heard a rich instrument like Saint-Sernin's would wonder why I have had some of my richest, almost mystical experiences listening to such a one.

I find it almost impossible to talk about music and how it reaches me. If I were a music scholar I could duck the experiential part and talk about the composition, comparing, say, Monteverdi and Vittoria, and remark how a particular motet could almost have been written by Gesualdo, which it wasn't. (These examples come from the program notes to a wonderful performance of a High Mass for Easter as it might have been presented in St. Mark's, Venice. The writer of the notes was not severely academic, however; he was able to exude over particular aspects of the works and say precisely why it was the jagged rhythm, the voices in thirds, the inverted melody that produced the marvellous effect.) I cannot do that. I can say, there, that bit now, that is what I love in this work, but I am ignorant of how it came to be so. Which rather leaves me speechless, or babbling, which is worse. I can say whether the music stirred up some feeling, some thoughts, some pictures in the imagination, some memories. But to say what the direct experience of the music is, there I am out of my depth.

I think I am not alone. Perhaps it is actually impossible to speak of music, except by analogy, to say with any accuracy what it is. Just as one cannot say how one knows the holy, but only what it does to you, maybe that is all one can say about music. Anything we do say is another one of those mediations that gets in the way of the direct knowledge one already has. Music has its own language; it does not converse with other tongues. It is the most holistic of all the arts, it gathers you together, picking up the fragments of daily life, putting them out of the way, and drawing you into itself. Somehow it brings heaven and earth together. Said a different way, it unites one's being with all that is glorious in the whole world. It is, to me, irresistible. Without music there would be no hoped-for world transfigured. There would be no possibility of the union of all people bringing creation towards a new day.

In the third century the Roman writer Martial called the city *Palladia Tolosa* (Toulouse the Wise is my translation) after Minerva, goddess of wisdom and music. Her patronage seems to have had fruitful, continuing results. This is the region where itinerant singing was ubiquitous in the Middle Ages, produced by everyone from pilgrims and troubadours to those defrocked monks and priests whose best-known lyrics have been given contemporary expression by Carl Orff in his raucous and rousing *Carmina Burana*. Troubadours flocked here, moving from court to court as they found or lost noble patrons. It was part of the so-called courtly love tradition that a noble should support the arts. Even the poorest viscount had one troubadour. Nobles higher up in power and prestige, such as the counts of Toulouse, had many. Probably the troubadour was most responsible for sustaining the mannered life of the court. One troubadour sang, "I love, therefore I sing," another demonstration that the medium is the message.

Today everyone sings in the streets, bars and clubs, since this is a university town. As we are walking home from the opera one night, a saxophonist is playing his heart out in a very small bar, with a capacity audience of twenty, inside and on the street.

The Halle aux Grains, a hexagonal nineteenth-century grain exchange building, is home to the fine Orchestre National du Capitole de Toulouse, whose current conductor, Michel Plasson, is one of the rising stars in Europe. We have heard the orchestra only a few times. It is usually on tour when we are here. Once it was an all-Ravel performance in which a blind Hungarian pianist played the Concerto for the Left Hand, magnificently. The audience would not let him go until he had played three encores. Plasson's conducting seems so uncontrived, the performance full of rapture and romance, a blend that Ravel achieves so well. Plasson has an idiosyncratic choice of programming, unusual for a major city. This year a concert advertised as "Homage à Casals" turns out to be, not music for cello, but an oratorio by Casals called *El Pessebre*, a work so loopy and seemingly directionless that only a skilled conductor like Plasson with accomplished musicians could bring it off, which he does. The Halle is intimate, the sound delicious. Musicians must enjoy playing here.

The Toulouse opera is as full of quirks and joys as the city itself. The performances are held in the unique Théâtre du Capitole, built in the sixteenth century, and redone in the eighteenth and twentieth centuries. It sits on the proud square that is the city's emotional and promotional centre. The first time we wrote for opera tickets from Canada, we were sent a note saying that all seats were subscribed except for those in Paradis. The price was right: very cheap, so we were delighted to take them. We found ourselves staggering up five steep flights of stairs, to be precariously perched in front-row seats with our feet dangling over the edge of what seemed like a sheer drop, as the other balconies are tucked back underneath ours. The French Paradis is just like the Canadian "gods" only much, much higher (and perhaps more theologically correct). But for someone who gets vertigo walking along a railway track, it was hard for me to concentrate on the opera.

I managed, though. It was Bizet's *Les Pêcheurs de Perles* (*The Pearl Fishers*), and my first reaction when seeing the set and the singers was to laugh. The costumes, the acting, and the colours of the sets were like something from a deMille classic, set on Coney Island, garish, silly and tawdry. The chorus, dressed in filmy uncertainties and wearing what looked like leis, behaved in a totally un-choruslike manner. Each person was doing something slightly different at a time when it was clear they were supposed to be synchronized and precise. One crossed and uncrossed her legs, another adjusted her lei on one shoulder, then the other. The women talked to each other when they weren't singing. To leave the stage, which they did several times, they had to descend what must have been a very narrow staircase at the centre back in full view of the audience. Their interminable exit was like a line-up waiting for the subway doors to open in rush hour.

But could they sing! The voices, one and all, were superb, and the sound in that building reached even unto paradise. Despite the deMille imitations, we were entranced. The next year by some miracle we had box seats at the first level. That time the company's budget must have been even slimmer; *The Marriage of Figaro* came with backdrops that didn't quite stretch across the width of the stage, so we could see cast members coming and going or standing in the wings, some clearly not realizing that we could see them. At one point the flapping door at one end of the set threatened to come off, but was pulled back by the hand of a hidden rescuer. The singing was gorgeous, and the acting comic and coquettish. The third time we went to the opera we were back in our old jumping-off place in Paradise. The theatre has just reopened after major renovations. I had hoped for an elevator, since non-subscribers to the season's program seem to be destined for loftiness, but alas there is none.

It is the sounds of the city that characterize Toulouse for me: musical, mechanical and vocal. One day, following along the fourteenth-century city wall, I come to where the Canal du Midi meets the Garonne River. The canal, with its grass banks for the towing crews to walk, seems like a pastoral vignette drawn from the days of its beginning. The river is quite another matter: broad, sweeping along grandly like a chauffeured dowager, it is banded by the hustling city on both sides. Far below me on the pier someone is playing the saxophone, jazzing up the river.

While the city pours out music of every sort, much of it forgettable, at its core it offers a sterling tribute to the high art of composition, in the opera, the symphony, the churches. I too have a taste for several musical genres, some destined to be here and gone, but in the end I always come back with deep relief and joy to the same fine cluster of works. Someone asked me recently what my "desert island discs" would be, and I said, almost in the next breath, Bach's *Mass in B Minor*, and Tallis' forty-part motet *Spem in alium*. After a few more breaths I came up with Messiaen's *Quartet for the End of Time*, and the trio from *Der Rosenkavalier*. Then, what else? Duruflé, and Bach, always more Bach. You can hear Messiaen, Duruflé and Bach often in Toulouse.

Another day we run into a large group of students parading down one of the main streets. It is the week before the national elections, and they are coming along in a leisurely manner chanting, "Down with racism! Down with Fascism! Down with the Front National!" and clapping to keep the rhythm. Serious intentions casually presented – how typical of this city.

Toulouse is home to Jean-Marie Le Pen, the ultra-right-wing leader of the Front National. It is he who wishes to keep France for the French, getting rid of foreigners (meaning mostly coloureds), and who seems to many to be the reincarnated spirit of Fascism. Toulouse seems to have the knack of drawing to itself all sorts of people who do not espouse the prevailing orthodoxy. After all, Le Pen does not have a majority here in this notably multiracial, university city. In the twelfth and thirteenth centuries it was the liveliest centre for the great southern heresy, Catharism.

There is a large sign beside the autoroute not far from Toulouse saying, This is Cathar Country. The immediacy of the sign might draw an unenlightened tourist into a shop to ask if you could buy some Cathars. History is tourism these days: if you've got it, flog it. Every paltry *tabac* shop in this region has a section of Cathar literature, in all languages. Having read some of these works, so highly charged emotionally that they would make Cathars of us all, I eventually came to historian Le Roy Ladurie's account, which corrects the balance, though my sympathies are still with the heretics.

Catharism is certainly a heresy, while a well-meaning one. According to Le Roy Ladurie, it makes use of Christian figures in a theological context that is so distorted it can hardly be called Christian at all. He thinks the source is Zoroastrianism, and suggests that it planted its roots so firmly in Languedoc because this was the trade route to the Middle East. The irony is, as he points out, that while Christians were trying to conquer the infidels en route to Jerusalem, the unwarlike Cathars from the east were spreading their quiet network over Christian territory. The paradigmatic two-way street.

The big problem theologically is that the Cathars (a.k.a. Albigensians, or Perfect Ones, as the truly committed ones were called) believed in a universe equally shared by a power of good and a power of evil. This world seems to have been the meeting ground, where the mixture of both is present. In order to banish the evil, one must abstain from any fleshly delights, meat and sex being primary, and pursue manual labour. The Cathars seem to have been morally upright, decent, mixed-up folk, mainly artisans, shepherds and some petty nobility. The most notable convert was the count of Toulouse, Raymond VI, and later his son, Raymond VII, but their motives included greed and jealousy as well as religious fervour.

I wonder about the church's reaction to the heretics. It seems that theological purity was not the chief reason for the pursuit that ensued, but more likely the fear that power and land would be lost. At any rate, that is why the nobles responded to the clergy's call to put down the heresy, plus the added attraction of receiving remission of their sins, and the spoils of the heretics. Davy says that intolerance was considered a virtue by such leading lights as Abbot Suger, who says of the murder of some infidels that they were "piously massacred." If that was the belief, then a lot of piety was being blatantly expressed in the *affaires cathares*.

Battles were fought all over our region and particularly to the south in the wilder countryside near Foix, a few days' march from Toulouse. The Cathars were pursued from fortress to fortress, where they holed up until their food ran out, the rats got into their wells or the sun dried them up. The leader of the church forces, Simon de Montfort, was, according to Le Roy Ladurie, as big a blackguard as all the sobbing tourist booklets make him out to be. He was in the fight strictly for gain and, it seems, for the pleasure of cruelty. One of the nastiest instances of his treatment of his captives took place at the castle of Lavaur, where he and his force put eighty knights to death, burned four hundred Perfect Ones, and threw the lady of the castle, who wasn't even a perfecta, down a well and stoned her to death. I cheered when I read that he had been killed by a woman outside the walls of Toulouse. Apparently even the pope had reservations about his drastic behaviour.

The final telling episode has the high drama of martyrdom, made especially poignant when one realizes that these were bakers and carpenters and such who were the heroes. In 1243–44 the last of the Cathars were besieged for ten months in their fort at the peak of great Montségur. Finally they gave in, and by an agreement made with their pursuers, walked down the mountain, two hundred of them, and into a blazing fire.

This was the end of the burning of Cathars, says Le Roy Ladurie. As a result of his heretical position and his capitulation, Raymond VII lost his lands and Toulouse its status as an independent power. To return to the church's good graces, Raymond had to forfeit land, money and his child, who was married off to Alphonse of Poitiers, brother of Louis IX. When Alphonse died in 1271, Toulouse and all the count's lands went to the kingdom of France.

Heresy had its impact even in Campagnac. Perhaps that is why I was drawn here. Our square used to have a pillory and a gibbet, I discover in the booklet about Campagnac. Around 1300, the seigneur of the area was given the right to dispense justice in the village. One brief note in the village records states that in 1315 or thereabouts, a woman was caught stealing the cloths from the church. Her hand was cut off and she was hanged. This startling episode set me to thinking about the little lives of the village and their part in the murky mulch of facts that is the history of this region.

I read that many of the Cathars were clothmakers, and that the word for "weaver," *tisserand*, was often synonymous with *cathare* at this time. Le Roy Ladurie says there was an expression, "Heresy is the daughter of wool" (not "the son," I notice). Could it be that the unfortunate woman was a Cathar, not a thief, and that the supposed thieving was the village's excuse to get rid of her? Or was she in fact a weaver, and therefore assumed to be a Cathar? By now the Inquisition had landed heavily in the southwest, the Dominicans and Franciscans moving methodically from village to village in their search for heretics. You didn't even have to be a heretic to get in trouble. If you refused to witness against one, you could be imprisoned. The poor woman's thievery sounds pretty suspect to me: who would be fool enough to steal the church's linens in this small place? What use would they be? Everyone would know in an instant who had done it.

I'm inclined to think that she was simply a weaver, and that the usual clerical argument was used to hang her: she is a weaver; therefore, she must be a Cathar. The church's linens have disappeared: she must have stolen them. It is precisely the same false logic as that in which the virgin was condemned on the grounds that she must be a witch since all women born of Eve are innately and insatiably lustful.

I must admit a sympathetic connection to this sinister business. I am from time to time an amateur weaver and spinner, and for much more of the time an unashamed heretic, even though that word is out of fashion now. My religious opinions have never followed the beaten track. I remember one hilarious occasion when a friend brought his dearest friend to visit me, thinking that we, being devoted Anglicans, would get on well. I can't remember what the subject was, or what outrageous theological line I tossed out, but it was definitely not orthodox. The visiting friend looked shocked, and with perfect seriousness said, "You'll fry!" I hadn't the heart to tell him I didn't believe in that procedure either.

So this daughter of wool seems suitably situated in a region that has over and over been resistant to orthodoxy, or to the prevailing powers. First there were the Cathars, then the Protestants, and in this century the Resistance fighters known as the *maquis*, who hid all over this countryside, fighting the Nazis and helping their intended victims to escape. The great difference between me and those earlier anti-establishment people is that they put their bodies where their mouths were, whereas I only sound off and try to lead a peaceable life. I have no greater courage than that.

I used to think it was mighty courageous just to speak what I thought. I was afraid of disappointing and perhaps losing my Christian friends if they heard my offbeat speculations. Also, I thought that if my well-constructed religious universe were to collapse completely, so would I. Consequently, I didn't pursue my ideas too far. I still have that feeling somewhat, even though the universe has changed greatly, and the friends have been more resilient than I gave them credit for. No one recently has told me I will fry.

I wonder if there is any relationship between my fondness for music and for heretical thinking. Such a discovery would make my life a little more coherent. The only connection that comes to mind is that I wrote the libretto, though not the music, for an opera about Florence Nightingale, a unique feminist whose religious position seems to me to be ambiguous. (I have been told by some who know me well that the Flo character I invented is remarkably like myself.) The basis for the opera, which was commissioned by the Elora Festival in Ontario, is a story that links Florence to the Reverend John Smithurst, rector of St. John's Church, Elora, during the period before the Crimean War. It was said that they were cousins who were in love, but because the church did not allow marriage between cousins, Smithurst became a missionary priest in Canada, and Florence turned to nursing. The fact that there is no firm evidence for this story made it both heretical and a good source for an opera, to my mind at least.

Both music and heresy have a certain liberty of thought, but behind that, both take off from a clearly established ground, exploring beyond the rules of the system. Music strictly by formula is dead: so is theology. Theology is something one lives and does, not a set of doctrines one studies. Just as the Bible is not an open book, neither is the history of the word of God both in and beyond Christendom. Interpretation continues, and theology must go on assisting with its inquiries.

In his closed republic, Plato condemned the poets, who are the musicians of words, because they innovated, and did not simply repeat the traditional knowledge. He feared that this departure from ortho-doxy could cause chaos. Troubadours were frequently Cathars or sympathizers, but after the persecutions began, some became Cistercians, one became a bishop, and a few became hermits. (Now there is an interesting connection to speculate about: music, heresy and mysticism in one lovely offbeat cluster!) It does seem that Toulouse, with two civic patrons leaning in opposite directions, has favoured Minerva over the orthodox martyred Saturnin.

Toulouse has always exerted a strong pull on my affections, ever since I first went there. It has taken me a long time to realize how that pull is significant for my spiritual life, but I am beginning to understand it. It is here that I discovered that I do not want to go urgently and directly to Santiago de Compostela. I know I will go there someday, but I can take my time about it, as that is not my real goal. It is now ten years since we made our first attempt to get there, and had to turn around at León because our time ran out. Or was it my ambivalence that stopped us? I cannot say. I only know this, that not being orthodox in anyone's terms, Anglican, or especially Roman Catholic, I was afraid to be disappointed or in fact put off by this shrine. When we started out at that time, I knew nothing about the saints, had a predictable distaste for the idea of relics, and a big chip on my shoulder about the paternalistic church. That was more than enough to keep me away from Santiago de Compostela. And yet...I wanted to go on a pilgrimage. All of this muddled thinking is beginning to come clear. I am still a pilgrim, beginning to make some sense of my repeated walks to the saints. Heresy and circular motion have their value, as I have always believed.

I am also convinced now that my heretical searching is a lot closer to true religion than is good old-fashioned orthodoxy. Religion today cannot be fuelled by faith in the old sense that revelation always takes precedence over reason, intuition and experience. Today true religion – that is, religion with integrity, without bad faith, self-deception – issues from the ability to believe and to be sceptical at the same time, and to be willing to drop those ideological statements that have been called "beliefs" when they run counter to reality.

Religion that is not based on lived experience, or reality seen in the light of revelation, is a lie. The expression "we are told that..." may do for children. We are adults who must not deny what is known through experience in favour of what someone tells us we are supposed to know.

Where the scepticism comes in is in the ongoing consideration of the relationship of our experience to revelation. Or should I say that revelation comes through our developing, faithful experience of reality. Faith is looking with eyes that are open to the divine eternal. Scepticism is refusing to believe that what I know now is all that there is to be known.

Religion in this way divorces itself clearly from ideology, which claims eternal status for a set of ideas imposed upon experience, not caring whether the ideas still fit, because the name of the game in ideology is power. Religion, when it becomes the shrine of power, is ideology and as false as any other.

I have lived more on the side of scepticism for some years now, exploring avenues and alleys, some of which have turned out to be dead ends. Many call for further exploration, and all of them have been worth the time I have spent on them. I have the feeling religion is finally catching up with my experience. How else can I put it? Some of the heretical thought is beginning to make sense to me. I have sorted out the relationship and now may begin to see wherein faith lies.

Heresy, music and Romanesque wedding cakes: no wonder Toulouse is my city for the present time. Its debt to the past is great: so is mine. My ideas wobble and go off-course, as did hers, and they probably still do. In the love of music and architecture we are temperamentally alike. How fortunate I am to have found her.

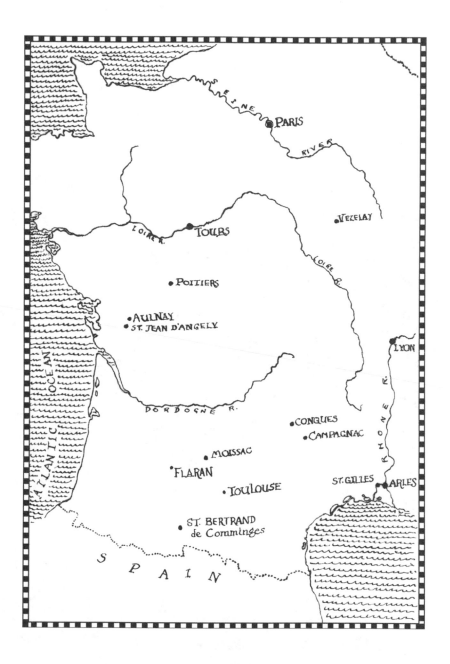

St Bertrand de Comminges

CHAPTER 8

— SAINT-BERTRAND-DE-COMMINGES —

Bertrand de l'Isle Jourdain. *Saint. b. circa 1050, Gascony, d. 1123, Comminges. Bishop of Comminges, grandson of count of Toulouse. Rebuilt the town and the cathedral which had been almost totally destroyed 500 years earlier. Reformer, miracle worker. Canonized 1175.*

There are some places I can never quite get a fix on. They elude me, not because they don't matter, or I have seen their mate a thousand times over, but because there's too much to comprehend. I don't mean that the treasures are all out there on display and that it is impossible to take in everything, like a civic equivalent of the British Museum. Rather, there are traces of treasures, hints of popular life, fragments of a long story that tease me into trying to piece them together, just as in doing so I realize I can never get it right. My assumptions are too narrow-minded, too romantic, and too ignorant. If I were the sole guardian of history, there would be no help for it.

Saint-Bertrand is one of those inaccessible places, inaccessible to me, that is, not to a proper historian. After my first visit I knew I had to go back: there was something I missed, and I thought it was visual. After my second visit I knew it was not. I know now that, although I will go back again once more, I will still come away unsatisfied.

When you first catch sight of it, it seems perfectly clear what it is you came to see. The site is like one of those places that abound in fairy tales, or any number of atmospheric medieval romances. The only difference is that on a steep pinnacle of a small mountain just big enough to hold it stands, not a crenellated castle, but a hybrid, mostly Gothic church. Behind it, playing their part as backdrop, are the lush green Pyrénées. Below on the approach side is the plain with a scattering of houses near the base of the hill. On the far side is the forest.

The day of my second visit is a perfect blend of sun and lightly brisk autumn breeze, ideal for perambulating, although too cold to sit outside for lunch. Cows are basking in the broad plain that stretches towards the hills. The first line of hills is called the Little Pyrénées, thickly padded with trees, some of which are showing tinges of fall colour. Behind them are the misty, powder blue peaks of the adult mountains, crowned with a light fringe of snow. Above them all, a halo of clouds breathes gently. The whole scene is not so much bucolic as silent. There is the presence of an absence.

The feeling is even stronger when we climb the hill to the centre of the village. It is as silent as a sci-fi novel where the inhabitants have all succumbed to a mysterious plague, a purple cloud. Practically none of the shops and restaurants are open; there is no one on the streets. There are no cars. We have arrived four days before the last tourist event of the season, the celebration of St. Bertrand's day, which is officially October 16. This year, Sunday falls on October 13, so a special mass and organ recital will take place then. After that everything usually shuts down. It looks as if people took early retirement this year.

The centre of the village is the cathedral, built in the only flat space at the summit of the hill. Beside it, there is only room for a small square, the *mairie* and the former bishop's residence, now a tourist office. Everything else is on a steep incline; the houses tucked behind stone walls too high to see over, even on tiptoe. You get a glimpse now and then through a cracked gate of a garden with a profusion of roses growing as far as the cliff's edge, and then nothing but the lovely Pyrénées behind. The village would make a perfect medieval film set: compact, isolated and intriguing.

Although an empty village in which people actually live is enough of an anomaly, it is not this that makes one sense an absence. On my previous visit to Saint-Bertrand there was no lack of tourists or of activities, and yet I had the same feeling, only a bit milder. What I'm missing are the real people, the founders of this place, genuine inhabitants who spent their whole lives here in activities that had no resemblance to the selling of cheap souvenirs and tough crêpes. There are layers and layers of them about whom we know little, and for whom this rather desolate, idle place would seem a travesty and a bad dream.

The first place to hint at what its story might be is the plain below, in the middle of which sits the trim Romanesque church of Saint-Just at Valcabrère, perhaps a kilometre away from Saint-Bertrand. Standing outside the little church with my eyes on the distant basilica, I realize that all the ground in between the two, and to the east, north and west of the mountain, was once populated by Romans, ten thousand or more of them. The city was founded in 72 BC by Pompey, and filled with his soldiers. Being on two good trade routes, it thrived until the end of the empire, when the Vandals sacked most of it. Still it carried on, and even though it was burned by a vengeful Burgundian it stayed quietly alive. Today the village contains two hundred and thirty people, survivors in the service of tourism, it would appear.

I wanted to see the excavations that have been made of buildings erected in various periods of the empire. What's left are stone floor plans, with a few of the walls partially reconstructed, but not very high. Far to the east of Valcabrère is the Forum, and near it the Temple and the Thermes, the baths in the city centre. I walk through the hot bath, another that I take to be the steam room, the cool bath, the cold bath and the swimming pool. There is also a change room and a court for exercise. I wonder if all the city councillors took a bath before or after their meetings, and if so what effect such relaxation would have had on their deliberations.

There is something odd about seeing heaps of pre-cut stones lying about waiting to be reused. There are piles of them, formerly part of the Thermes, now about to be placed in the same building which has been turned into an artifact. I find this objectionable, though I'm not sure why. I'd love to see the baths as they were, but that can never be. So I'm inclined to vote for constructing a maquette, and leaving the ruins as they are. Because the baths seem so contemporary, like a downtown spa and health club, I could imagine the citizens in the forum debating this issue: to rebuild or leave as is. I can't say what their decision would be.

Not far away in space, though over three hundred years distant, I walk through the nave of a fifth-century Christian basilica built, curiously enough, after the Vandals had sacked the town. It had been an important centre of worship once, being about 45 metres long. Now the walls are low enough to jump over, and the grassy nave is occupied by sarcophagi lying around carelessly in no particular arrangement. Apparently the church served as a mausoleum later on in its life, but no one seems to know how long that life extended.

Here are the only traces of another group of Saint-Bertrand's citizens, even their graves displaced. Because of the context, this seems to me to be a sad place, in contrast to the liveliness of the Roman quarter. Still, there is a distinct air about the basilica, a sense that there are stories being told here, if only one had the right sort of hearing.

John Berger, wearing his cap as cultural historian, says, "How easy it is to lose sight of what is historically invisible – as if people lived only history and nothing else." It takes a lot of effort to keep in touch with the past, whether it's the march of world events, societies and sensibilities, or the historically invisible such as the personal past of places, times, perceptions and people. You have to read, go to libraries, look at old maps, unearth old documents, photos and drawings. If you are lucky you can talk to the remnant of previous generations, put on a tape recorder, use the Internet. In other words, you have to want to spend some of your precious free time on it, rather than taking your ease by the fire or in a lawn chair.

The past is, of course, all around and beneath us if we know how to look. Archaeologists and geologists can tell us plenty about the historical underground and its layering. Every city I have visited, more or less, mentions the Roman or pre-Christian ruins that have just been found underneath the church, the city square, or somewhere else. If you live in a place where what is new seems to count, or what is coming down the line, it is more difficult to stay connected to the past. My children know very little about their forebears, even their names or where they hailed from; they never asked, and I never volunteered when they were young. Now it's almost too late to pique their interest; it will have to wait until they are my age perhaps. I, on the other hand, was fed repeatedly with stories about my great-grandparents, my great-aunts and uncles by my maternal grandmother Smith who relived it all in the telling. She would help me to get to sleep at night (this was my excuse and she bought it) by telling me about her childhood. In the daytime I picked up random snippets about who we were, as she reminded herself, I suppose, that she could make up in ancestry for what she lacked in worldly wealth. As the only child of an only child, I am beginning to feel it is up to me to carry on the family narration.

If you are not lucky enough to have relatives with the knack for storytelling and the memory of what Uncle William's father's profession was before he came out from the Old Country, and whether he married a woman from the elder or younger line of the Aberdeen So-and-sos, there are stones. Stones are enduring, visible links to the past if only we can read them. Gravestones are a starting place. They circumscribe one's personal history, but say nothing more except, in the case of those carved with sentiments or ornament, something about the attitude to life, death and public emotion of those who installed them.

To the Romanesque builders, stones were already objects of memory. They were in love with antiques, the statuary and architecture of the ancients, and incorporated portions into their new buildings. Charlemagne brought back from Rome and Ravenna chariots full of old marbles. Figures of classical heroes underwent a name change with baptismal effect: Marcus Aurelius became Constantine, for example. I have seen a Roman sarcophagus built into a church wall somewhere, ancient columns used in a porch. The twelfth-century philosopher/teacher Bernard of Chartres described what this meant: he was the first to say, *pace* Newton and Coleridge, "We are dwarfs perched on the shoulders of giants. Thus we see better and further than they do, not because our sight is keener or our height greater, but because they carry us in the air and raise us up to their gigantic height." These builders and thinkers saw themselves as moderns, building on previous greatness, never reactionary but moving forward. The Church had in the main refused to do this, believing there could be no progress, no alterations in beliefs over time, eternal matters having been settled once and for all. St. Bernard of Clairvaux disagreed: "Truth is the daughter of time," he said. Architecture went along. What masons couldn't find among the ruins, they copied from old manuscripts or drawings of classical motifs. The language of Roman architecture was repeated in their domes, vaults and arches; all the while the designers continued to work out improvements in stress, height and light.

The reminders these building stones offer to the student of history seem a long way from the private and peculiar history of families, of Uncle George and Aunt Ida. There are exceptions: I remember bringing home a photograph of the bosses carved in the roof of a cloister of Canterbury cathedral bearing the arms of local families, and showing it to a friend whose knowledge of heraldry is enormous. He gave me a genealogical account of the families whose arms were there, what their occupation was, their relationship to each other, who was next in line to inherit the estate, and so forth. The one thing he couldn't tell me was their names, but he said that with some detective work these could be found too.

The other sort of exception is more idiosyncratic, and for me, strangely evocative. When my aunt Doris died, her lawyer gave me what personal documents there were left, including a photograph album which I glanced at then and put away, only to forget about it for the next eighteen years. Last month I took it out. It is a collection of tiny black-and-white photographs, mostly from the years 1938 to 1950. All the early ones come from her years in France, at Auxerre and the Sorbonne. Some show the school where she taught, her friends there, the picnics they took together, and the usual group shots standing on the school steps. The rest are tourist photos taken on holidays with nice-looking young men in baggy, tweedy suits, and women in clunky shoes, tight-chested dresses and boat-shaped, fedora-like hats. I remember my mother in similar outfits, and even at that time thought the hats were ridiculous.

The surprise was in the buildings they photographed. There was nothing very unusual about most of these grand historic French sites. They are the ones the discerning tourists head for sooner or later. It was perhaps the timing of my discovery. The first photo Doris put in her book was of Rouen cathedral; this was the first cathedral I ever laid eyes on in France. The next snap was of the château at Villandry taken from the terrace; I had taken almost the identical shot just the month before. It went on: Azay-le-Rideau, Chenonceau, the usual Loire glories, until I turned the page and found myself first in Venice, then Florence, finally looking over the piazza in Siena. As I write, Bob and I are planning this very itinerary in the fall, in the same order, and will probably photograph the same buildings. This is not an unusual thing to do, but somehow there was a special family connectedness about finding these pictures right now. I said to Bob, "Doris looks just like Sarah here," but he disagreed strongly. All the same I kept getting a sense of my aunt and my daughter, joined by blood, somewhat by appearance and temperament, crossing over the lines between death and life, thanks to those stones, those remarkable objects of memory for centuries of pilgrims, for my aunt and now me. It brought me to tears, but for what I don't know. Eliade, the great scholar of the whole realm of myth and symbol, says that ancient peoples would return regularly to the sacred stones of their ancestors for renewal.

I am not alone in my fascination with ruins. Perhaps it is part of that feeling that crept in as the 1900s rolled over into the 2000s, a nostalgic looking back, because we are afraid the zeros would cancel out memory and force us into a blank-page mentality. Perhaps too it is because ruins tell us something we cannot learn anywhere else. A church with crumbling walls open to the sky and grass for a floor says more about mortality than a solid one does. A Roman temple whose only remaining architecture is four fragmented columns on a platform asks questions about the relative nature of religion, alive and defunct. These ruins give me more desire to fill in the gaps than if I were to find the works complete.

When you stop to think about it, how many things are really whole? Not us: we begin dying as soon as we are born. Buildings start to decay immediately, plants get diseases and bugs eat them. This sounds like the old sixteenth-century cry of mutabilitie – change and decay in all around I see. People do not usually think that way now, though. While gradual rot is occurring, our minds still think that things are whole. At what point do we change our idea of their state, and call them ruins? I think it is when one cannot make sense of them anymore. For instance: a sick body is ruined, because the decay is meaningless. A broken building, whose form cannot easily be understood. A garden, when the chafers and slugs have munched and shredded the plants. A book, when water sticks the pages together, or mould attacks. A love, when self-hate breaks into it. A god, when she or he does not live up to our expectations.

Some people today would say yes, that is exactly what has happened: the image of God has taken the wrong shape and it is diseased, stained and shrunk. I don't think so. I think we must allow the form we now need to emerge. We have matured as far as our cosmology is concerned, and we lack a sufficient image for it. To put it another way, we need new eyes and ears, though we are not yet ready to use them. We are stuck bewailing or trying to support the ruins instead of looking and listening afresh. Perhaps that is why these ruins seem to contain a lost presence.

The new church, the one built on the hilltop in the twelfth century and onward, is not a ruin. Because of the popularity of St. Bertrand, who as bishop managed to revive both church and village, the cathedral as it was then was enlarged and heightened twice. Today, undamaged by the Wars of Religion, it has an oddly complex shape, partly owing to the change of taste from Romanesque to Gothic, and partly because of the problems of building on such a high, narrow site. The bell tower, usually over the porch, had to be placed over the nave to prevent the whole structure from falling down the hill, or so they say.

The tympanum over the main door is the only one I have seen that shows the Adoration of the Magi. It is a lovely one, with the angels floating above the simple scene, making a warm welcome to this rather isolated church. Mary holds her little boy – he's no infant – on her lap to receive the wise men's gifts. Joseph is, as usual, away from the main action; here he holds his staff with one hand, the other hand raised in gratitude to heaven. For once he has something magisterial to do, even if he is isolated.

There are three more wonderful things about this church, which is in many other ways interesting but not engaging. There is the most exquisite organ screen I have ever seen, built in the corner of the nave, and raised high up on carved wooden Corinthian columns. It is a fantasy, a child's architectural delight, a Renaissance tour de force. It houses a splendid organ, and is one reason for an annual festival of recitals that is held in Pyrénées churches along the route to Santiago de Compostela.

The second and even greater splendour is the choir, with its carved Renaissance stalls. The choir and sanctuary are totally closed off from the nave and the ambulatory, so the faithful congregation could hear the monks singing, but see nothing. Meanwhile the monks could feast unseen on the carved figures that adorn the backs of the two rows of stalls behind the misericords that also gave them support during the long hours of prayer. If they flipped up the seats of the misericord they could see even more interesting carvings underneath. There seems to be no comprehensive plan for these stalls: most of the saints, famous and little known, are there in low relief. There is a group of personified virtues; and all the Sibyls are represented, although no one has so far explained their presence sufficiently. A few biblical scenes are done in high relief and attached to the ends of the stalls. Then there are the figures of the misericords, which are scatological to say the least.

Most of the guidebooks do not bother to mention these, thus avoiding the question of why they are there. There is, for instance, the carving of a naked young man, squatting with his legs far apart, defecating. Parallel to that is a frontal view of a naked woman whose outspread legs end in webbed feet, and whose vagina is covered up by a devil's mask. The book whose subject is the choir stalls says that these figures represent the real world, in contrast to the above-board figures who are supposedly in the ideal world. The carving of the woman is titled "The infernal seductress." There are other scenes that seem to me to be gratuitous involving nakedness and odd performances, two in which a clothed adult is beating the bare bum of a young person. These are a far cry from Gurevich's "nimbus-crowned magicians" I am accustomed to finding in the house of God.

The final treasure of Saint-Bertrand is the cloister, which is attached to the south side of the church. Its rarity is owed not so much to its sculpture, although there are some notable capitals, but to its situation. Without enough room on the top of the hill to enclose it with other buildings, it sits on the brow of the hill, its outermost side a picture window from which to view the mountains and the dense, cool forest below.

The forest is too big a symbol for me. Dark, undifferentiated, labyrinthine, prehistoric, it perhaps holds as many memories as there are trees, too many to be uncovered in a lifetime. This particular forest is singled out by one event: on a plaque near the town wall below the cathedral, passersby are asked to remember with gratitude the *maquis* who were killed there during World War II defending "the honour of France."

When St. Bertrand came to rebuild this town he probably had to hack his way to it. Forest covered a great deal of what is now France, particularly since much of the arable land had been abandoned over the centuries. Time and again, farmers were forced to leave the land and flee from the waves of foreign and neighbouring invaders. Some of the forests belonged to the kings who used them as hunting preserves. Many were used by seigneurs and free citizens for grazing pigs and cattle. People did live in the forest, says French historian Marc Bloch: woodcutters, bark strippers, gatherers of wax and honey, hermits, hunters and charcoal burners. In places it was thick and uncharted, dark and difficult to pass through. It was here that the pilgrims were at risk from its chief tenants, wolves and marauders.

Cold and starvation took many pilgrims, but the wolves, murderers and robbers were even bigger threats. Sometimes they were so terrifying and impossible to get rid of that the only recourse was to cut down the forest. In the meantime, plenty of pilgrims came to grief. Stories of attacks by wolves and bandits must have circulated constantly. The first story would have made me turn back, no matter how glorious the reward at the end of the journey. But then I value life for its own sake, which was not the case, it seems, in the Middle Ages. Death was not so fearsome as it was to become later on; rather it was a longed-for destination. Perhaps medieval people rationalized that death by wolf's bite or brigand's stick was a quicker way to the eternal desirable than just crunching along in the old, miserable way. How impossible it is to imagine how people thought whose lives were driven by different needs, overriding beliefs and underlying folk fantasies. Who can say, for instance, what hell or heaven really meant to a farmer, a pilgrim, a seigneur or even a monk? Or a woman who might not even have a soul? If I truly believed that, I might have headed out for the nearest wolf.

Our own neighbouring forest, the Grésigne, has its own bloody history of massacres, robberies and other disasters. One of my friends will not walk in the forest, or drive through it, for that matter. He fears its ghosts. Some of the ghosts are noble, though, martyrs whose patriotism is difficult to comprehend by someone who has never had to stand up for her beliefs to the point of death. During World War II our region produced many *maquis*, who carried out brave, foolhardy attacks on troop installations and convoys of German vehicles, and recaptured whole villages. Foolhardy, because the villages were quickly recaptured by the Germans and the *maquis* were hanged. These young men marshalled in our forest before being sent out on daredevil jobs to Albi, Gaillac and nearby villages, for instance. There is one story about a group of forty of them waiting in ambush for three hundred Germans, ten trucks and two huge guns. Two men were captured, six others were killed, but they managed to disarm one of the guns and three of the trucks. They killed sixty Nazis. The two who were captured were let go through the intervention of a nun with the German doctor, and by means of threats from the local *maquis* leader, who said all the German prisoners would be killed if the two were not released.

Forests in many parts of southern France were shelters for Jewish refugees, though I don't know if any were harboured near here. At first they were hidden with local families until they could be passed along the escape routes of the Pyrénées, including those that ran through Saint-Bertrand's forest, to Spain. In 1943 when the Nazis reneged on their pledge to leave southern France unoccupied, Jews were forced to find better hiding places. My friend Georges Jeanclos, the sculptor, who was hidden with his family in the forest near Clermont-Ferrand, has described what sort of life it was. He told me that they had to keep on the move frequently, making occasional forays into the villages for food and water. They ate forest food: mushrooms and berries. They were always on the alert for Nazi vehicles coming in their direction. One day when he went down into the village to get water, he saw some SS soldiers, and he ran away so fast he spilled most of the water. He was eleven years old. It was the forest that saved the whole family, however, all ten of them.

I heard a lecture recently by Ivan Kalman, an anthropologist, who said, "Monotheism was born in the desert, not in the forest," and I thought, that is true, but what difference does it make? Probably a lot. For one thing, if you are going to require an image by which to represent the divine, there are not many to choose from in the desert. Wind or breath would be the strongest, and so that is what the Hebrews chose. Islam and Christianity divided their attention between the unrepresentable and the human. If you think about the shamanistic tradition of the Inuit, where the landscape is almost as bare as the desert, there are very few images to carry the spiritual. Polytheistic religions are not from the desert. The sources of imagery in a green and fertile world for expressing the most deeply felt meanings are vast.

When Christianity came to Europe it changed the pure monotheistic strain we inherited from Judaism. In France, where forests have taken over much of the land that was abandoned during wars and invasions, the worship of martyrs and saints flourished. When it begins to flavour Christianity I don't know, but certainly by the Middle Ages the saints are the focus of worship and the direction of that worship comes mainly from the monasteries; many of them, such as Sainte-

Odile in Alsace or Conques, are situated on isolated, forested heights.

I am working on an idea that, though incomplete, goes something like this: In a country such as France, where the predominating sense of wilderness is the forest, not the desert, a sort of Christian polytheism has arisen. The sacred creatures that are venerated are not the wood nymphs or water spirits of older religions, who each in their peculiar way participated in and assisted the rhythmic flow of nature. They are saints, superhumans with power to control the other forces of nature. This odd manifestation in a religion that is theologically monotheistic occurs owing to the meeting of earlier pantheistic understandings of the world with the dominating hierarchical attitude of Christianity, which gives pride of place in nature to humans, under the authority of a supernatural deity with fully human characteristics. It seems that there is an environmental variable – the forest wilderness – that helps to account for this unusual situation.

The view from the cloisters at St-Bertrand looking down into the lush forest below where the *maquis* were shot is beautiful and serene. On that day it would have been both beautiful and ghastly at once, but no one would have noticed the beauty. Finally it struck home, what my mind had always found difficult to grasp, that we can never really know the land. Not only does it hold its secrets, like the massacre of the resistance fighters, closing over them like leafy trap doors, but it too changes over the centuries in ways we can only speculate about. We know that forests were cleared, then left to grow again, then turned into arable land, and so on. But we do not know how the contours changed, what the winds did to the land, the vegetation. The forest below me only seems eternal; actually it is probably nothing like the terrain the pilgrims went through. Perhaps it is unlike the forest the *maquis* knew. That is part of the reason why the forest as symbol is too big and unfathomable. It is forever changing.

Running through the shards and hollows that history has left here, there is something, a slight whiff of a breeze, steady, almost imperceptibly stirring the air. I have waited patiently for years for the breath of God to blow towards me again. (Lovely old symbol.) I am not usually very patient. The urge to push on is probably my worst fault, at least I think Bob would say so. I cannot wait for people to get going, to make decisions, for parcels and letters to arrive, for visitors to get here. If they're slow or held up I can get frantic, sometimes furious. I really wish people would make up their minds as fast as I do, and then do what they say they will right away. If they are faster than I am, though, I get frustrated trying to catch up. In any case, hurry is the watchword.

For a few years I felt a crucial absence I did not at first want to admit. The academic study of religion had broadened my theological base, bringing new questions as well as volumes of new information. I felt alive, immensely stimulated in this process, so much so that I didn't realize until much later what had departed. I cannot think of a better word for it than devotion. The love I had been left with was of the ideas of God, not of God in person, not a God who could be addressed. I had no problem with this: I believed God was alive and growing livelier all the time. I knew I was, so that was the proof.

Then as my reading, thought and experience took me further afield, I began to realize what I had lost: the old image of God, the comprehensive cosmology. I was terrified at the thought of it. My entire world's stability depended on the sacred universe that I had erected, and that had been erected for me. Without it, my whole understanding of self in relation to the world might collapse, or so I feared.

It took a long time for me to gain my equilibrium and learn patience. I kept reminding myself of a time many years earlier, when I had complained frantically to a friend that a very significant group of Christians to which I belonged was in danger of breaking up. His dry remark was, "Don't think the Holy Spirit is going to stop working just because you do." It made sense then, it does now, and it has kept me patient.

I want so badly to make a connection, to say "You" to the universe, to the divine: however, meeting my need for a deity on the World Wide Web is hardly a reason for the existence of same. Yet there is this little breeze, this hint of something that causes me to say aloud, "When will I find You?"

I guess I've just put myself on the line. I must be cautious, even overcautious. I still don't know about this You, what that implies. It has been a long, long time, and my patience is running out. Why don't I try Anne's wager, and simply keep saying "You"? Hang the consequences. I can always fight back, reason, rationalize, deny. I'm good at that.

In this strangely silent place, empty yet full of mysterious ambiguity, far, far removed from the everyday, there is room for the petulant question, the trembling bravado, and the hope that some breeze from the forest will bring a response.

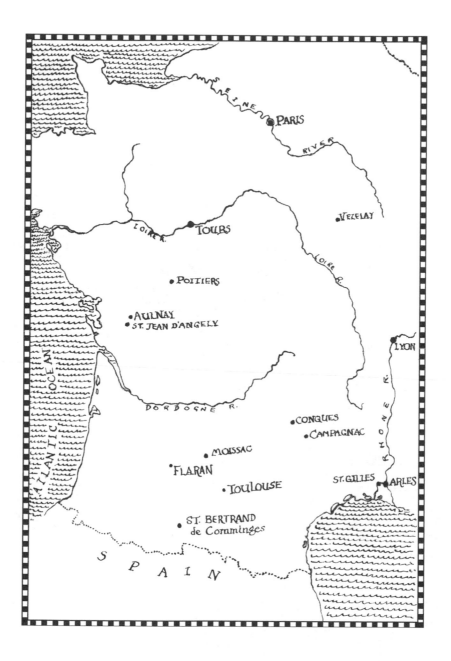

Fassade St. Gilles, am Rhone zerstört 1870

CHAPTER 9

— ARLES, SAINT-GILLES —

Trophîme. *Saint. b? d. second or third centuries. One of the first bishops of Arles. Patron saint of the city. Legend confuses him with another Trophîme, cousin of St. Paul and companion of Mary, Martha and Lazarus, who is thought to have converted the city. Relics venerated.*

Cybèle. *Goddess. Origin Phrygian, adopted by Romans. Also known as the Great Mother, Mother of the Gods. Greatest goddess of the Ancient Near East. Consort Attis. Shares with Jupiter power over plant, animal and human reproduction. Her temple on top of the Palatine hill is the site of games in her honour.*

Mary, Virgin. *Saint.*

Gilles. *Saint. b. circa 700, Athens; d? Hermit, but having directed the king to build a monastery, was persuaded by him to become its abbot. Among his many miracles: gave his tunic to a diseased man, who was cured by putting it on; cured a man bitten by a serpent; calmed the waters when sailors were caught in a tempest; raised the king's son from the dead.*

A moment to savour: on an old cobblestone road below the parapet a dog the colour of stone walks with his mistress dressed to match. I am leaning on the Roman wall facing the most splendid silhouette of Arles across the Rhône. The light is pale, tingeing the stone but not irradiating it. On the far shore one woman walks the *quai* as I do. It is impossible to see whether there is any traffic because of the height and overlapping of the buildings. All seems calm. The water, a soft grey-blue, moves amiably along, the dog sniffs a fascinating Arlesian scent, and an arrowhead of swallows flaps its way swiftly down the river.

Like Poitiers, the skyline is pinpointed with churches. I see four Romanesque buildings, perhaps a fifth, the pointed spire of what might be local Gothic, and one whose origins defy me. Time stands still. There is nothing I must do except look and wait. Over there on the other side, not a soul moves up or down the pyramids of stairs cut into the embankment wall. No one possesses the river and the river possesses no one. It is quiet on this side too. Only a gardener leaves the house behind me, his arms full of unwanted excess oleander branches. What serendipity. One of the many church bells has struck 7.30; the others, disagreeing, follow soon after. Time for repast after reverie.

This is such a different Arles from what I have seen before. I came back because I thought I should. All pilgrims come here, no matter what their stripe. I thought there was probably more here than the attraction of an arena and an important church and bulls and cowboys. You cannot, you should not try to tear it apart, its history, its archaeology, its peoples. It is as complex as personality stretched over character. Maybe that is why I am coming to love it. On all my other visits I saw it as a site of specific treasures or curiosities. The first time I came it was the antiquities, excavations, fragments that intrigued me. Another time I came for the medieval buildings, walking only those streets that led to churches. A visit with my mother was to see museums. Once Bob and I and the children came in from the country for Sunday dinner: Arlesian sausage, heavy, fatty and over-praised, I thought.

This time I came for the city, and it rose to answer my question: are you a living place or a conglomerate of sites? What a difference one's intention makes, depending on whether you want to isolate and focus on one aspect of a thing, or try and take a view of the whole. Is this the problem with my religious search; I am asking the wrong questions, walking too narrowly, tunnelling my vision? I argue with myself: yes, but there are serious questions to be asked. I'm not going to go all flabby, talk about spirituality in a vague way as if it could absorb anything and then equate the result with the faith once delivered to the saints. Counterpoise: that's beyond the point. I am trying to reinterpret that faith for me, a very-late-twentieth-century woman in a post-ecclesiastical age. It is not easy. I get confused. I am never spiritually (here's that word!) or theologically satisfied, much less certain. I do know that the journey, this pilgrimage, is being guided, not by the usual kind of direction I give to my own activities wherever possible, but by something else that is inward, unsure, yet content to be allowed to choose where and how I will go.

Arles is a survivor who has turned her battle scars into urban benefits. From my brief reading of her history, I gather that she must have been at times the most powerful, and at other times the most beleaguered, of southern cities. Today her suffering does not show, nor of course her triumphs. She is probably, with the exception of Paris, the French town with the longest and best pedigree. Inhabited by Celts, who were preceded by an unknown primitive lot, she became early on an important commercial port, shipping out cloth and bringing in Eastern spices. She was one of the imperial cities founded (that is, taken over and allowed to live) by Julius Caesar himself. She owes her all to this: that in the major battle between Julius and Pompey, she backed the winner. Marseille, her neighbour, chose to support Pompey, and lost out. Arles became the seat of civil and later religious power, capital of the realm known as the Seven Provinces. Her thriving economy was maintained, based on the sale of salt and the control of navigation up, down and across the Rhône.

Arles is a study in human geology. You cannot go anywhere without bumping into, or falling down in, one of the layers of the ancient city, old even before Caesar came. Excavations seem as ubiquitous as parking lots, the one often beside the other. You become aware just how old stones can be as the one you stumble on may just have been part of a fourth-century villa. Recycling expresses its true meaning here: nothing is ever really lost. Arles today is full of good shops, eateries, bars and entertainments, just as it has been off and on over the centuries. One really isn't surprised that its great sports stadium is 2000 years old.

I have decided to let the city tell me where to go. It strikes me as weird that the first place to come to mind is the cemetery called Alyscamps on the edge of town beside the old via Aurelia. Though I did not know it at the time, this was to be the first hint of what I was later to discover much more fully and delightedly.

You have to pay to go in here, a small amount, to walk along this broad, tree-shaded *allée*, alongside which the tombs are set in straight lines. Alyscamps, a corruption of Champs Élysées, Elysian Fields, must once have suited its name, for this is the only remaining fragment of a necropolis that was as large as the city of Arles itself. Burial place of notable citizens from time immemorial, it became a Christian site in the fourth century. Christ himself is said to have appeared at its consecration. Then, starting about four hundred years ago, it was completely emptied, the city deciding to offer these fine carved Roman sarcophagi to kings and prelates for use in their palaces. My guidebook says it became a veritable stone quarry. Sometime in the last century, after most of the cemetery land had been taken over for new construction, a few tombs were rescued and returned here.

Here they sit, the empty kernels of the dead, split open, their lids missing for the most part or married to a different tomb. I wonder about their desecration, the one part of their history that is not discussed in the books. All those sarcophagi, each one of which must have weighed a ton or more, were opened, broken, and the contents removed. By whom? Fanatical Christians removing the pagans? Citizens who wanted to sell the tombs removing the Christians? They lie in the sun like discarded molluscs on a beach.

Most of the writing on the tombs is difficult to make out, and almost all the carved images have been effaced by time. There is one coffin lid that makes me pause. At each end, facing outwards, are two massive heads, their hair falling in neat coils down to their shoulders, their eyes fearful and their mouths agape. It seems that the fields ahead may not be as blissful as the heavenly tourist guides suggested.

The long walk beside these tombs is peaceful. The other visitors speak quietly, as we all head towards what is left of the church of Saint-Honorat at the far end. There's not a lot: a fragment of the nave, open to the sky, then the sanctuary, with its central crypt, some side altars, a transept and what may have been a baptistery or vestry. A side chapel off the nave, and that's all.

The square lanterns allow plenty of light to the sanctuary, which is supported by round columns, the biggest I've ever seen – three or four people joining hands might encircle them. The mixture of buildings added over centuries comes together like a well-made patchwork. There is the warm, tawny colour of the restored sections of the centre, the grey sediment of the past covering the side chapels and transept. Although empty and unused and partial, it has a feeling of holiness much like that of Saint-Hilaire. I have the urge to touch everything, and I do, running my hands over the rough surface of the altar whose carvings respond better to touch than sight, they are so worn. I dip my fingers into the stoup empty of holy water. The place is holy enough for me without it. On another altar I trace the shape of a long cross. Another has a well-carved façade with Christ standing between two apostles, speaking the gospel. The central crypt is simple and empty; on the walls are carved the arms of many nobles. All these stones seem important, necessary to the church's existence, oddly compelling for mine. Nothing is superfluous, yet nothing matches.

Why do I feel so at home in a place that is empty even of its dead? Funnily enough, it does not seem empty at all, not like the Christian tombs at Saint-Bertrand, where all the souls had left along with the bodies. Here the souls have gathered, Christian, Roman, Gallic, Celtic, Phoenician. This hallowed site grasps me, beyond rational thought. Could it be because I am writing this on All Saints' Day?

It is strange to see a young woman with her child in a stroller going through the building at about the same pace as I am. An older couple follow hand in hand. My guidebook says that Alyscamps has long been a popular place for Arlesians to walk.

Arles is the smelliest city I have ever been in. In the morning it is cool and humid and I wear a long shirt. By noon the flies are biting, and even carrying the shirt feels hot. Then I smell the city, a mixture of sewage and industrial fumes, plus something repellant and unrecognizable. I thought it came from inside, but when I move out of doors I find it there, just as overpowering. Fortunately the sounds of traffic, business and people conversing draw my attention away from it. I am sitting in the place de la République eating a Camembert sandwich. Everyone around me is licking ice cream, chocolate and pistachio. The town is bulging with tourists, but people seem to take them in their stride. I say this because the tourists and locals occupy the same places. There is no dedicated souvenir and trashy gift sector, except for a few small stands around the arena. In the square I am in – a polygamous marriage of Roman, Gothic, Romanesque and Baroque architecture – people are going about their various ways, at the city hall, in the museum, or just hanging out. Many, both locals and tourists, are contemplating the façade of Saint-Trophîme.

What is so unusual about it is its resemblance to a Roman triumphal arch; most guidebooks compare it to the one Augustus built at Glanum outside present-day Saint-Rémy in Provence. You mount a broad set of stairs to encounter a massive colonnade in whose embrasures are standing figures in high relief. These are surmounted by an arched doorway enclosing a tympanum depicting the Last Judgment. Above that a peaked cornice rather weakens the effect of a mighty imperial edifice. It is still more than enough to assure you that the church is solidly founded. The carvings are in good shape: hieratic figures with oversized mythic creatures at their feet. I particularly like Hercules fighting the lion. Here the allegory is of strength conquering sin: poor old lion, he does get shunted around between the good and the damned. How could sculptors be so fickle?

Inside it is a very soberly constructed church, fully fitted out with doubled vaults, and eight chapels around the apse. I am glad to see that for once Joseph, the forgotten man, has a chapel to himself. In the Nativity scene on the outside of the building he is shown rather forlornly sitting at the side, head resting on the hand that holds his staff, the other arm on his knee. One chapel is filled with nineteenth-century gilt and glass reliquaries from which assorted unidentified bones peek out. Not a great turn-on for me and, since no candles are burning, presumably not for anyone else either.

The church remembers its antecedents, which is a nice touch. Several fourth- and fifth-century sarcophagi stand there, one of which offers two sculpted scenes in unusual parallel: Cain's and Abel's offerings to God are paired with the Magi's presentations to the Christ Child. I wondered if, since Cain's gift was turned down by God, one of the wise men's had been a reject too, and which one would it be? The building does not however give any hint that in its place once stood a temple to Diana of the Ephesians.

This was a major stop on the routes to Santiago de Compostela, Rome and Jerusalem, yet apart from the façade it seems almost humble for such an important centre of pilgrim activity. It is squeezed in between two other buildings, with no breathing space at all. Had there been no signs I would not have known about the gem of a cloister hidden away next door.

You go up a tall marble stairway to reach it, and enter what seems like a roof garden, because you are two storeys above ground. Two sides of the cloister are Romanesque, two Gothic, with a large grassy court in the centre and oleanders planted along the edges. The columns have the usual biblical scenes, hard to see because they are so shaded and are much tinier than in Moissac or Saint-Bertrand. There is a warmly encouraging St. Jacques, wearing the pilgrim's short tunic and carrying his familiar pouch. Another staircase takes you up again to an opening in a wall, and out you go to the roof of the cloister, where I was greeted by the noonday Angelus. My timing is so haunted with antique reminders! No one here stops moving. I sit down and observe the cloister below, the wall of the ecclesiastical enclosure next door, those oleanders, blooming cerise and pink. Of course the sun is out, it must be about 25°C, and the clouds are pretty and piffling. This pilgrim is beginning to think the cards are stacked, but for what I cannot say.

As I move about the city I get the sense that something is building, or I am building something. I am quite prepared to take responsibility for it, whatever it is. On a lovely square at the height of town I come upon the church of Sainte-Marie-de-la-Major. It is a small, worshipful place awash with Marys. In one corner there are three: two sculptures and a painting, each showing her holding her child; in one she wears a crown and a lovely Renaissance dress. At the north side is a magnificent bronze Virgin and Child, which has been removed from some even older site. This church has known much devotion. It was built, on this choice piece of ground, on a site formerly occupied by a temple to Cybèle.

Going across the city, outside the old town, I head for the new Musée de l'Arles antique, a place of fascinating artifacts, plenty of good information, and lots of space in which to ruminate about it all. Here I learn by looking something about the transposition of symbols, and how one religion builds on the back of another.

The tombs show it best, as the old Roman images give way gradually to Christian iconography. I watch the disappearance of Cupid, called Amour, and the arrival of cherubim. On the Roman tombs of the High Empire, winged Amour drives a horse-drawn chariot taking the dead soul "beyond," as it says. On a fourth-century Christian tomb, Amour has become a cherub, a naked child, but the winged adult angels are clothed. On a second-century, still pre-Christian tomb, Amour holds a garland in the centre of which is the winged head of Medusa. On another sarcophagus I find the winged Medusa described as the protector of the tomb, one who wards off evil. This is a far cry from the Medusa we are used to hearing about, the ugly Gorgon with the snaky locks whose glance turns everyone, good or evil, to stone until Perseus does her in by looking at her in a mirror, rather than directly. A subsidiary legend says that she was a beautiful girl whom Athene jealously turned into a ghastly horror. This is how it works, one religion damning the previous one's gods.

In this airy, pleasant new space it is possible to spend hours without realizing it. I stay all morning discovering the local deities. I find a tiny seated figure of the mother goddess, undated but surely very ancient. I read that she, Cybèle, is often shown seated and holding a key to unlock the powers of vegetative reproduction. It makes me think back to the figure of Mary in Poitiers holding the keys to the city. Crowning the end of the vast gallery there is the copy of the tenderly beautiful Venus of Arles, larger than life. The original was given to Louis XIV for Versailles. There is Apollo, the god of poetry and music and of the theatre of Arles, whose remnants are still impressive today. Apollo is represented here on a sarcophagus with his customary two bay trees, whose leaves were chewed by his companion *la Pythie* (python) to assist in prophetic trances. Good, mystical serpent. There are figures of Minerva and Aphrodite, much revered in this town.

What have I learned? That the world is full of amazing things, that goddesses were very much in the forefront of life, along with the gods, that Cybèle came to help the Romans in Gaul as did Minerva, Aphrodite and Diana. That Medusa is a protector, not a witchy demon. That pearl necklaces aren't a grandmotherly idea, they are prehistoric.

After the resounding presence of all these wise and powerful women, it must have been very hard for the Christians to assert the importance of Mary the Virgin. While virginity in goddesses was considered "powerful magic," it didn't go hand-in-hand with humility or obedience. Was there a great gap between the decline of the goddesses and the promotion of the virtues of Mary? Were all held in esteem for a while? It seems from the appearance of the fourth-century tombs that both mythologies continued to exist together. Medusa appears on Christian tombs, and Amours sit side by side with angels. These early tombs have no representations of Mary as queen-qua-goddess, as she was to appear later on.

Are we returning to those civic and honourable virtues the Greeks and Romans assigned to their goddesses, in declaring that the virtues latterly ascribed to Mary are not the right ones today? I don't mean in the new thrust of goddess worship, which seems to be mostly concerned with woman as nurturer, mother earth. What I mean is that in the secular world of women's politics, we value wisdom, power, insight and love. We need to draw these virtues out of ourselves, not ascribe them to a cast of antique women and then worship them. I cannot help remembering, though, that these goddesses are also bad-tempered bitches, jealous wives, murderous, vengeful mothers. Maybe I should just think of them as fellow travellers.

The image of Mary as soft, humble virgin of few words supported piety appropriately in earlier centuries, but today she seems waxen and wan. She needs to get a life. I hope an expert in Mariology is taking it on. My only thoughts about her lead me to want to link her with Cybèle, great mother. The difficulty here is, Mary is only indirectly a fertility symbol. It is her Babe who, to put it that way, gives life to a deadbeat world. I suspect most women today would prefer to associate themselves with Cybèle.

How is it possible to incorporate the "new" women – Cybèle, Minerva, Aphrodite – into the Christian understanding of life and salvation? The answer I come up with immediately is: they are instruments and because they are part of Western history, they can be assimilated, because they already have been! Every time a new world hypothesis heaves into view, it condemns and tries to cancel out all the previous ones. Still they are there, in the mix that is the collective consciousness, even if unremembered. Just because the ruling power vetoes their presence is no reason for them to go. And they do not.

Here I am, two millennia later, looking once more at these women, these figures, freshly, but not for the first time. As goddesses they are of no particular interest to me. As possibilities towards which women reach, as moral models made acceptable again as the twentieth century turns into the twenty-first century AD, they are what is needed. Jung says that the mother archetype is the symbol of transformation. I accept that possibility.

These goddesses have been lurking about all along (every Grade 7 class covers Greek and Roman mythology at the very least), but we have not taken them seriously. There are excavations of Venus figurines in central France, crude but compelling fertility figures. Images of mother goddesses have been found in many places. The official word has been that they are pagan: that is, outmoded, useless, powerless, even malevolent. What this means is – O wicked patriarchs! – that they must not be allowed to intrude. While I understand and acclaim the ancient Hebrews' need to be different, and hence to bring forward the all-powerful god at the top of the pyramid, why not keep the pyramid too? It does seem like the simplest, easiest way to establish the hegemony of Yahweh.

We are not in the same situation as the Hebrews, defending themselves against other more powerful cultures with their great, established set of deities, and trying to keep their community intact. We are, though, once again a small group paddling upstream and trying to stay afloat and together. There are no influential gods against us persuading us to change our worship and give them their due. If history is any teacher we have two choices: the first is to hole up, put blinkers on and recite our beliefs in the same credal language as the past, ignoring the culture and discoveries of the last two thousand years. The second is to do what the Romans did when they came to Gaul bringing their gods and those of the Ancient Near East with them: make the best use of the collective wisdom of the time to advance religion and therefore culture. We do stand on the shoulders of such giants: it is foolish to think of them as ignorant creatures of a legendary age that is dead and gone.

I love Arles. It is a city neither pompous nor self-conscious. It is self-centred, of course, just like all French towns. It prides itself on rice, which grows in the famous marshlands of the Camargue to the south of town. It takes history in its stride. If ruins are discovered where a parking lot was planned, skip the parking and uncover the treasures. Cut a hole in the floor of the lobby of a first-class hotel, cover it with glass, to show the ruins of a Roman villa just unearthed below. Arles is not purist: every period shows up somewhere, in bits and pieces. So fix some of the pieces, leave the rest. Take pleasure in it all, ugly or beautiful, broken or whole. How this smacks of the realism that is one's everyday life. Arles is a lesson easy to digest. In its innocent lack of awareness or posturing, it leaves room for me to ponder and perhaps grow in understanding.

I love its casual people and style; the modest art shrines showing with an even hand folk art, antique sculpture and Picassos; the singular churches; the mixing of ages, so well accommodated, which gives one the sense that history is lively in all directions; the strong, inscrutable goddesses, the fiery Medusa, the serene Aphrodite; the sense of welcome, of inclusiveness, rather than a dictatorial showmanship, frozen in time, narrow in thought.

Finally I love the contrast between the great river, sweeping all along, and the city collecting, refining, breaking down and rebuilding all the detritus of history, and keeping what it can. The river tells me that much more fell into the depths of forgottenness than was saved on the banks, becoming part of the universal oblivion that we will eventually share.

Arles says there are battles to be fought and won and lost, ruins to be swept away, new eras of prosperity in life and faith to appear. Then there is the river, putting all those thoughts and ideas into everlasting perspective.

A few kilometres to the west of Arles, probably a day's walk for pilgrims, is the small, sleepy town of Saint-Gilles, which in medieval times had a population of 30,000. This was an extremely important halt for pilgrims, the Cluniac abbey church having been consecrated, like Saint-Sernin in Toulouse, by Urban II on his grand tour. St. Gilles' reputation for working miracles was so outstanding that supplicants came from all over Europe. In 1085 a delegation came from Poland, bringing as a gift a gold effigy of a newborn child to ask the saint to grant the king a son. The church has been often destroyed and rebuilt. Still it is imposing, as you look up the steep, broad steps to its wonderful façade. Time has had its way with the sculpture, and yet the immediacy of some of the original work remains. There are some vignettes here that one doesn't usually see on the church front, the tender one of Jesus washing Peter's feet, for instance.

The outside walls are composed of stones squarely and cleanly cut, with hardly a sign of mortar between them. Unfortunately the interior fabric of the building hasn't fared so well: the first time we went there we were told that the upper level, the church proper, was not open to visitors, being *"en mauvais état."* If we would wait till 2:15, however, we could see the crypt for free. We had lunch and returned.

An old fossil of a woman exuding no human warmth at all came with a fistful of keys to undo the padlock and chain around the gate leading to the crypt. She was so crippled, her movements so slow that I thought we'd never get down the steps together before it was time to close up. The crypt is very broad with a high ceiling, but no interesting capitals. Here are the relics of St. Gilles, discovered in 1865 under a pile of stones, where they had been hidden for fear of heretics (a story with a familiar ring to it). Today the relics repose in a stone sarcophagus once used by Gilles himself as an altar. Leaning against the iron railing surrounding it are many walking sticks and canes, evidence of the saint's special gift. I thought how ironic it was that his tomb guardian had received no help from him. If she had known of the customary procedure followed by medieval sufferers, she'd have banged on the sarcophagus with her stick and told him to wake up and do his duty by her.

There are profound metaphorical possibilities tied into this great section of the route, called the via Domitia. Stretching between Toulouse and Arles, it was a very early section of the road for pilgrims going to Jerusalem. Then when Santiago de Compostela became the rage, the human traffic went in the other direction also. Travellers must have exchanged stories, warnings about hazards to come, the same way we flash our lights at oncoming cars to warn them about speed cops. I suppose they sent messages: tell my wife you saw me, and that the cloak she made is torn already, but the shoes are holding up so far. Say the cough remedy I brought is no good, but there is a chap with us who has a better one.

Did they, I wonder, brag about their particular journey, or the merits to be gained by going towards one shrine or the other? Were pilgrims bound for Santiago de Compostela considered second-class compared to those headed for the Holy Sepulchre? Did they tally up the number of relics they had visited, the feast days they had enjoyed, the miracles they had seen or heard tell of? I am sure they did. And did two friends, perhaps – here is where the metaphor comes in – decide to take off in different directions, each convinced that his or her way was the more salutary?

This is I suppose what really happens when old friendships die out: we change direction, sometimes like on the via Domitia, going in exactly opposite ways. Recently a forty-year-old friendship, after many jolts and restarts, finally croaked its last. I am not sure if either of us was completely happy to let it go. For four decades, we had travelled joyously, sadly, seriously and humorously over what seemed to be the same path, sharing religious, intellectual, musical and artistic views. There was a rare, mystical insight that we never conveyed to anyone else, because we thought they would not understand. For a time we were the best of friends. But in later years it was becoming clearer that there were divisions of interests, and the one supposedly unbreakable strand of understanding was getting thinner and thinner, until finally it snapped. She became more reclusive, living more like medieval people in the immediacy of life, at a country pace. I became more worldly, captivated by plans, thoughts and doings, citified. Except when in Campagnac. Our directions have reversed, or so it seems. Yet there are times when I think thoughts that I am sure only she would understand. Perhaps we will meet again along the route, one going east, the other west, and have some stories to exchange.

The second time I came to Saint-Gilles the upper part of the church was open. The interior is unremarkable except for the massive pillars supported on two-metre square plinths half a metre high. You would think the building would be here to stay, but in fact half of it was removed after the destruction ensuing from the Wars of Religion. The church was once vast, now it suits a small parish.

An organist plays a series of unrecognizable works using the same unappetizing stops for all. There is surprisingly little reverberation for such a tall stone place.

So why does it happen that in this odd place and at such a time, I have a change of heart, a tiny discovery? There is a sweet nineteenth-century altar figure of Mary and child, both of them crowned and dressed in gold. Very nice, not gaudy, but more like porcelain dolls than sculpture. I am nevertheless moved to light a candle, a fat one that looks as if it would last all day, perhaps even into the night. I don't know why, I tell these figures. Then I knew I was accepting my role as one of those ordinary, stumbling, unsure pilgrims who have poured into this sanctuary for hundreds of years. Perhaps many have had my thoughts, doubts, questions and waverings off the path.

(The organist is taking his wavering way through the Hallelujah

Chorus. What is it about this piece that they all want to adapt it only to ruin it?)

Then came the counter-argument: I must not fall into the old trap, becoming a follower of Mary the humble, and so forth. The answer to that, of course, is that I am the woman I am and no other. It is as this person that I can participate in the life of faith, however slantwise I may be. (The organ is unbearable. I must leave.) I do not need a woman as model, although it would not hurt. I need to keep my integrity, my questions, the lot. It is a different way than that of obedience and humility, which in me only fed a masochistic tendency I have happily outgrown. All the warts will not disappear, but some have faded. Others emerge under pressure. How helplessly angry I feel when my way is blocked, for instance. I am sure that this will not stop.

I come out of this place as a silly pilgrim, but full not empty. My needs do not drive me. I do not require an eternal hope to fill the lack of an everyday one. I am not ambitious to be an ecclesiastic, a religious or a saint. What do I desire? The truth of faith. Knowledge of the divine. The eternal quest pursued, the light becoming stronger. Peace at last, I suppose, but I am aiming for joy.

Arles and Saint-Gilles showed me that a living thing can emerge when you combine symbols from different pasts. The façade of Saint-Gilles has the look of a Roman theatre, but the frieze recounts the Passion of Jesus and the right-hand door has the Crucifixion in the tympanum. Below are the saints, below them mythical beasts support the columns, and along the base of the pillars are the signs of the zodiac. All this and heaven too, because in the centre is Christ in majesty with the four evangelists' signs beside him.

Beliefs overlap. They do not go in direct lines like theological arguments, or like pilgrimages to far-distant shrines. They walk about just like my pilgrimage and that of countless others, absorbing riches wherever they may be found. Eventually the time comes when another authority, another overwhelming cosmology appears, doing its best to remove all traces of previous inhabitants. Then rituals are established, beliefs are formulated as creeds, pilgrimages go in straight lines for a time, and the world seems simpler. I cannot say that I am looking forward to this with unalloyed pleasure.

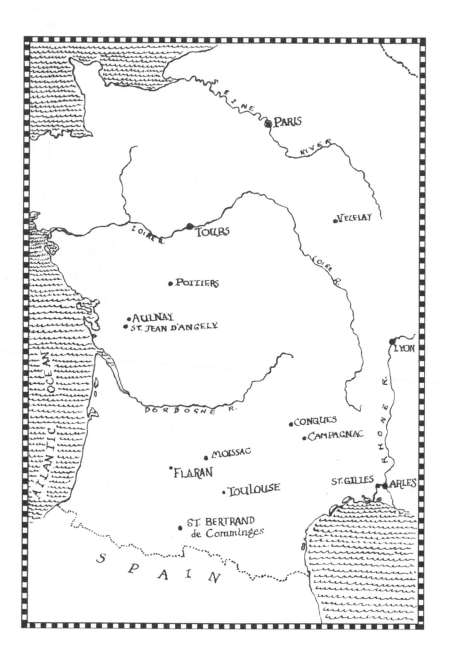

CHAPTER 10

— CONQUES —

Foy. *Saint and martyr. b. circa 191, d. 303, Agen. Condemned by the Roman governor to be beheaded and burned. Many miracles attributed to her. Patron of the blind and of prisoners.*

It is high time I introduced Mitsi, because she has been along on many segments of this pilgrimage. She rattles, she is leprous, her stuffing is coming through. She is a foreigner who has had so many homes she doesn't know who she is any more. She is twenty years old and can handle curves like a juvenile. Her name is Mitsi Mitsubishi, and she is a veteran pilgrim if ever there was one. Her second name is Galant, and it becomes her.

Our son Ian bought Mitsi in the Netherlands through the good graces of a friend's mechanic there. He and his friend drove her to Greece and back to Rotterdam. At that point he estimates that the speedometer had rolled around twice. We bought Mitsi from him for $1100. That was fourteen years ago. Since then she has been to Florence and back, and on every pilgrimage excursion except the ones into Spain: we decided to spare her, and us, the Pyrénées. Every time we come here we think this must be Mitsi's last year. Every time she starts at the first turn of the key. Considering how little she is used, perhaps her actual age is only about twelve. Even so I doubt she will go very far into this new millennium.

Mitsi has been to Conques many times, rocking and rolling over those rough roads, and into the hairpin turns that are bound to discourage all but the truly pious or snoopy from going to this remote village, even by car, let alone on foot. Going up from the river valley to the summit of the hill, I think there certainly had to be some relics to cause droves of pilgrims to climb up here in worn-out sandals.

Conques is truly my fantasy within a fantasy. In the middle of this luscious land I dote on, there is still another place even more desirable and precious. Set in a cleft in some rather savage-looking hills, about as far away from any two-bakery-, one-butcher-size town as you can get in this hungry country, is this storied village of four hundred and thirty souls. The site having been deliberately chosen from the beginning as a refuge from the world, it has been hidden for most of its twelve hundred years. The only exceptions have been that glorious century, mid-eleventh to mid-twelfth, when it became a goal of pilgrims in its own right as well as a major halt on the route to Santiago de Compostela – and today, when the touring pilgrims come again.

It was one of the first places we visited after we moved in to Campagnac, and before I had any clear notions about looking at pilgrim places. It's a good two-and-a-half-hour drive from our house over tortuous roads, so the idea must have been compelling, however it arose. What I remember of the first encounter is falling in love with this silent, forlorn and yet strangely spiritual place. I didn't know about the relics here, about the hordes who came for them, about the little girl martyr whose church is the focal point. It was simply that this was sanctuary, drawing one deeply into oneself, for good or ill. Not the abbey church alone, but the whole coming together of hills, town and twisting river.

The first time we came we found a high place underneath a towering crucifix on a hill across from the town, where we had a picnic and looked dreamily at Conques. Then we went back to town again to try and tackle the church.

In the square, a cartoon figure of a rotund monk in brown habit and sandals is standing in front of the church door. With a very long stick he points out the figures on the tympanum to a group of people craning their necks to see. We find out later that he does this every day at the same time, for any who happen to be there.

The Last Judgment that is modelled in the great tympanum shows with precise architectural thoroughness what certainties are in store at the end of time. The three-stage universe is presented, not geographically but as it spiritually should be, with all activities radiating from Christ in the centre. The angels above support the cross; on the middle level Christ blesses the elect on one side, and on the other angels hold back the devils and the damned from approaching him. The lowest tier shows the saved on the left (Christ's right hand), each neatly housed within an arch of his or her own. Opposite them the damned are jumbled together into a crowded place, the ultimate tenement house. As with most pictures of hell – Milton's comes quickly to mind – the activities and expressions of the damned are far more interesting than those of the blessed. No one has ever been able to find a satisfactory answer to this problem. Of course, if theologians had permitted sexual delight to be included in their vision of heaven, the iconic balance would have shifted joyously towards the side of salvation.

According to Gurevich, an "eschatological frame of mind" was prevalent from the late eleventh through the twelfth century, which puts this tympanum right in the middle of the period. One of the medieval monk-scholars had the temerity to explain the Last Judgment by saying that "the damned are created for the elect's sake, so they can rejoice in their own salvation"! In his view God is merciless and implacable. Later on, as one might well have guessed, there is a sort of theological softening; the devils disappear, and the fight for souls becomes an abstract one, between good and evil. The church introduces mediations between the soul and the gates of hell: the idea of purgatory, and the power of intercession through the Virgin and the saints. All those devils, whom Gurevich calls a "medieval virus," go back where they came from.

For all the grandeur of the tympanum, the church is simple and relatively unadorned. As the books on Romanesque architecture tell you, its design is the same as the four other key pilgrimage churches, in Tours, Limoges (both destroyed), Toulouse and Santiago de Compostela. Being the oldest, it was probably the model for all of them. There is nothing whimsical about the form: the churches had to serve the needs of the parishioners, the monks and the pilgrims. One solution was that of Saint-Gilles: build an upper church for the parish and a vast crypt for the pilgrims. The other was the Conques model, which most builders copied: a partially enclosed nave for quiet worship, surrounded by side aisles leading to an ambulatory around behind the altar. Off the ambulatory one could add as many chapels as necessary, five usually, but here three. If you needed a really big space, you could make wide transepts so crowds could watch the mass being celebrated, as they did in Saint-Hilaire. Of course how you designed the building depended upon where you were going to put the relics. In Saint-Sernin, where there were many, the crypt was built under the altar, making possible a smaller circuit under and within the ambulatory. Here at Conques the relics had, if you can bear it, a mind of their own, which finally determined their resting place.

The patron saint of this marvellous place is St. Foy, a twelve-year-old girl of Agen who was killed in AD 303, shortly before Constantine ordered the conversion of his empire, and the possibility of martyrdom grew slight. I cannot think of another child martyr with whom to compare Saint Foy, but she certainly had presence, and the traits of a spoiled child, which in a sense I suppose she became after her death. When the abbey church became too small to hold all the pilgrims and still allow the monks to pursue their meditative ways, the abbot decided to build a special oratory for the relics alongside the church. Saint Foy would have none of it, and refused to be moved from the centre of things. The plan was dismissed.

One of the most famous treasures in France is her reliquary: a half-human size seated figure, clothed completely in gold leaf, and adorned ostentatiously with large cameos and semi-precious stones. Although it is supposed to represent the saint, the head, which clearly belongs to a different body, is that of a Roman emperor, massive and unwieldy on top of this child's figure. The effect is striking, though, and Foy would have loved that, for she adored jewellery and glitter. One story told of her is that when the countess of Anjou wanted an heir, Foy demanded the gift of two enamelled and jewelled sleeves, after which donation the countess produced two children. Foy seems like a juvenile Cybèle. Her reliquary is kept today in the treasury off the remains of the cloister. How she would have fought that move! She now keeps company with a fine collection of Carolingian and later gold-and-jewelled containers for sacred objects.

History as we know it today is so boringly concerned with getting the facts straight, with supportive evidence and all that. The story of how Foy's relics came from Agen to Conques avoids all that extra baggage, and is more significant as a result. It is said that (to be fair, one should really introduce this kind of sacred-historical tale that way), the monks of Conques were very keen to have some relics, but none had come their way. How the desire for the fruits of tourism does make cheats of us! One of their number, along with a servant/companion, disguised himself as a pilgrim, and went off to the monastery at Agen. His humility and outright piety so endeared himself to the monks that after fifteen years there he was put to guard the holy relic. One night, when the monks were at supper, the two interlopers stole St. Foy's body and rushed off to Conques. The year was 866.

It does make you wonder a little: pilgrims weren't known for staying around any shrine, for the idea was to keep going; and Agen was on the route to Santiago de Compostela where, just a few years before, the body of St. James had been rediscovered and piously installed. Surely the monks would have penetrated this disguise, as there were plenty of *jacquards*, false pilgrims, about. Also, in the decades just before the theft the Normans had invaded the southwest, and settled in nearby Toulouse. One art historian says that the monks of Agen probably removed St. Foy to Conques for safekeeping. (Presumed sequel: Conques was so blessed with miracles that they refused to return her.) Having said all this, and knowing that there are seventy-nine other relic-stealing stories similar to this one, it is still fascinating to think about the complex spiritual makeup of someone who would wait deceptively and piously for fifteen years for his heart's desire.

St. Foy's particular skill is in curing bad eyesight, and in helping prisoners to escape. Perhaps that's because she herself was "liberated" from Agen. She also escapes from her glassed-in embrasure in the treasury at least once a year, on an occasion when her delight in adornment is surely satisfied. By sheer dumb luck (?) I caught it once.

Several friends were visiting over the Canadian Thanksgiving weekend: among them a professor of veterinary science, a noted silversmith, and a medieval historian who invests all things sacred and secular with a vivid, sparkling aura. They decide to drive up to Conques on the Sunday, Margaret insisting, against my protests about preparing dinner, that I must come along. I wouldn't it put it past her to have the gift of presentiment. When we approach the village it looks utterly abandoned, not a soul around. Then we find the parking lot, packed with cars and buses, and realize as we walk along the street that everyone must be in the church. We can hardly get in the doors: it is packed with people standing in the aisles, and up the steps. At the far end are many heavily embroidered priests taking part in the service, and at the right-hand side of the chancel, a famous figure is enthroned, surrounded with vases of flowers. I say to Margaret, "She's there!" and, knowing immediately what I mean, Margaret inches her way along the side aisle to the front, intending to absorb every drop of this momentous experience. Our other two friends, less taken in by medieval hocus-pocus, give it a few minutes and go out exploring the town. Margaret and I revel in the whole glorious event, the saint's patronal festival, which spills over afterwards into the square, the bishop shaking everyone's hand, and all having a fine old time.

October 6 is St. Foy's day, and one year I am going to be there in time to see the procession that brings her reliquary from the treasury into the church. I wonder what sort of music she likes? Tambourines would not be out of keeping, especially if they were gold.

The next year we miss her festival by four days. It's a bit like arriving at a party when most of the guests are gone and the dirty dishes are lying about – whatever the cause, this time Conques exhausts me. We spend an hour or more wandering around the almost empty church, and afterwards over coffee I can hardly stay awake. Why should this visit to a cherished, familiar place be so stressful? I wonder. The day is beautiful, there is nothing wrong or out of place about it, and yet I am drawing a blank. There are no religious insights, no romantic overtones, no new thoughts, nor even a trace of the usual pleasure. It is almost as though the dear place has given me all it can, for now at least.

Admiration for the builder is the best I can muster. The effect of the church is so cohesive, the two types of stone with their pale yellow and rose cast softening the severity of the form. Light suffuses the interior, unimpeded by Pierre Soulages' strange but beautifully suitable new windows, a commentary on the lines and material of the building. The light inside and out is golden-rose like the stone, showing nature basking like a lizard on a stone wall. The light is slowing down, though, as are the tourists: restrained, serious, all of them French, not foreign. There is a kind of nostalgia about this visit that I am not prepared to let emerge.

What I am really missing of course is much greater than the joy of a sparkling, devotional festival day. It is the loss of what Northrop Frye calls the Great Code, the whole, encompassing story that makes sense of the Christian life, both belief and behaviour. Without cosmology, not just the Christian one, but any at all, it is difficult to "believe in" one's own action, to justify it to oneself, never mind others. What does it mean if I say I have integrity, but cannot say what it is I have integrity about, or why that matters more than other things about which the idea of having integrity doesn't even come up? You really have to be a pretty clear-headed humanist, such as Camus was, to be able to stand up for integrity and name your reasons for it. He made it into a moral conflict, almost like the old one between God and the devil. Here you were, declaring the worthiness of the human cause and prospect, over against a world deemed to be absurd. Defiance came with this view, and determined activity, plus a rich belief that despite the odds, life was worth the trouble.

It is very difficult to sustain such a position, and few but heroes do so. I try to imagine Camus heading up the Absurdist Humanist Party and squashing the Front National but I cannot. What I think we need is a shared description, a new code, of the universe that allows us to go on our merry or miserable ways without inordinate fear that everything could come apart at any minute. The state didn't work as a substitute symbol system, and neither will a belief in the brother-and-sisterhood of nations.

For women it is just the right time to rediscover the goddess. Those who have done so are in a far better position than men who have turned away from the catholicity of the Christian universe, and have nothing to put in its place. Just as this old universe is tottering and about to tumble, these women say, you've got it all wrong; the structure is crumbling because it was upheld by the wrong sort of deity. Before and beneath all this triumphalism that developed from the patriarchal religion of the biblical Jews, there was a deity of quite a different sort. Behold, she is still here, undaunted, roused from her prison where she was buried like the man in the iron mask! From this re-emergence has streamed new religious consciousness, new prayer, new liturgies, new hope and joy. Since orthodoxy is a bad word to these keen religionists, the feminist awakening has gone off in many directions, some of them kooky, some perhaps not.

My problem with goddess worship is just that: worship usually implies belief in the factuality of the adored and the failure to recognize that the goddesses and the saints are symbols, not idols. I don't say that it is impossible to worship while at the same time realizing that it is the reality shining through the symbol that matters, not the object/figure/image itself. It's just damned difficult. It means that eventually you get a division between the plebs, who worship idols, and the intelligentsia (i.e., the experts in the religion), who adhere to the "higher" truth, just as you get in the major religions. Then, you are on the fast track to becoming a religion with its own brand of hierarchical structure.

I am such a Pollyanna. I really do wish the world were infused with goddesses, and gods, and then my friend John could write a new Ring cycle with St. Foy as child-protagonist, and we'd all dance around and give thanks that the world was properly looked after again, and we could stop worrying. Sadly, the best I can do is say, I am glad there were goddesses once, and saints, and holy people. Otherwise we would not be the sort of people we are today, but perhaps something far worse.

The fall is a funny time of year to celebrate a child martyr. Everything is coming into the yellow leaf, moving quietly towards sleep time, not as in Canada with the trumpeting of Jack Frost. There are chestnuts all over the roads, crunching fiercely under our tires. We pass old men collecting them, a black-and-white terrier foraging alongside. The pile of grape skins beside the *salle des réunions* in Campagnac is enormous; it has been a very successful year, at last. The *vigne vierge* on the house is turning red by infinitesimal degrees, the colour stealing along from the front of the house towards the door.

I am lulled by the sympathetic magic of the season to think of my life as fading gently, leaf-like, curling its edges, drying its veins, losing colour, until finally the brittle leaves break off and are discarded. What a lovely way to go – yes, Dylan Thomas, I'd rather have it this way. The trouble is, I remember the spring and summer, probably not as they were, of course, but at their imagined best. It might be fine, this aging business, if I hadn't known another time that seemed more liberated, more profound. Now I feel encircled by my body's foolishness, its slow healing process, by my inability to think of five different things at once as I used to, and by anxiety about the future. In ten years I'll think of this present time as happily free of...who knows? I haven't given my anxieties such concrete form yet.

Even though I am now officially old, I find it difficult to think about because, despite the slowing-down process, I do not see myself as old. An old woman? No. Miserable, negative thought. Oak trees, Roquefort, Burgundy, Bordeaux and Cognac are praised for their age. People by and large are not. Oriental carpets and silver mellow luxuriously with age. People give tiny ransoms for eighteenth-century porcelain, which hardly shows its age, though it boasts of its pedigree and workmanship.

Then there are the old masterpieces, which gain in stature as they age. Was the Parthenon always so prized? Perhaps not in the same way. Literature doesn't age, one thinks, but George Steiner, that multilingual humanist, says that we appreciate language less and less, as its meanings are swallowed up by our mediocre intentions and failing apperceptions.

Do we get better perhaps as we age? Am I so focused on the withering-up of the physical functions that I miss something here, perhaps a special quality of grown-upness that took many years to polish?

I suppose that one of the qualities that attracts me to Romanesque buildings is their aging. Look at a restored capital and compare it with one that is decaying, soft at the edges, missing a few parts, quite dilapidated in fact. I love it this way, although it can be terribly frustrating to find one where so much has eroded that the scene is undecipherable. Here is aging in its romanticized mode, suggesting to the mind inclined to nostalgia a past that never was: but then, all pasts never were. Even though I know this, I love touching this past, feeling it give way in the present, so to speak, yet being there still like a ghost, not itself, but a memory of itself.

There are three little theories about growing old that I think about, trying to decide which one will win out eventually. The one I favour depends on my mood, the weather, the company I've been keeping, and the success or failure of present ventures. In other words these aren't theories at all, but sentiments so deeply felt they seem to be a true account of how things are. The most rational, I suppose, is the one Muriel Spark shows us in *Memento Mori*, where she deals her cast of octogenarians some wicked, ironic blows. Spark tells us that you're going to be in your old age just the same as you were before, only more so. If you were anxious when younger, you'll become paranoid. If you were saving, you'll become miserly. If you were scrupulous, you'll become fanatically so. It figures: after all, why should we be different, instead of caricatures of our present selves? One or two of her characters are actually pleasant. They are the ones who take aging in their stride, as they have everything else in their lives. None of these people are ennobled, though, by the loss of hair, teeth or breath.

My second notion is that you will be struck down or weakened in that area of your being that you were most proud of, or most concerned about. A beautiful woman gets breast cancer, Beethoven goes deaf, a philosopher gets Alzheimer's. Is this silly fatalism, or a deep psychological motivation, or none of above? I keep sneaking in the odd conjecture as to what I'm likely to fall prey to, but don't dare chance a statement. Gurevich says that one of the popular medieval conceptions of hell was that the punishment exactly fitted the crime. I guess I've answered my own question.

The third is the belief that Browning's Rabbi Ben Ezra espouses: that old age is joyous, free of stress and strain, leaving one space for looking and loving. Ripeness is all. It's my fantasy, of course; who would choose otherwise? It is one I believed in when I was thirty but now I'm not so sure.

On this latest visit we come to Conques on the tiniest twisting lanes that take us over hills and into valleys twice as numerous as on the usual routes. On a hilltop approaching the village we have our picnic. The mist prevents us from seeing across to the furthest hills. In good weather you must be able to see for 30 kilometres or more. Below us is Noailhac, a miniature Conques, with fields of cows and forests filling in the rest of the picture. We eat across from the tiny chapel of Saint-Roch, whose slightly overdone plastered yellow figure with his dog supervises and guards all pilgrims en route. The *randonné*, the walking trail, goes by here on the way from Conques to Figeac. Just below the chapel the path is lined with fourteen stone crosses at about nine-metre intervals. I hope it is liturgical, not funerary.

There are figures and wayside chapels dedicated to St. Roch everywhere because he is the patron saint of pilgrims. The story is, back in the fourteenth century, Roch was attacked by brigands in the forest and wounded severely in the leg. A dog came by and, taking pity, went back home and brought him a loaf of bread every day until he was well enough to go on. Why wasn't the dog beatified since he was the hero? Had this story been 100 percent folk tale and not Christianized, the dog would have turned out to be a human/divinity in disguise. The best that public approval can do is represent him beside St. Roch in every carving.

All this beauty, this history, these questions, even the taste of picnic strawberries dipped in *crème fraîche* drunk with a little *perlé* wine, fade into the background before the assault of the wind. The temperature is down – it must 16 degrees. We are wearing our windbreakers, which do not. The sky is a softly misted blue, the clouds are long gauze bands and streaks, and the sun is constant, keeping company with the wind which blows steadily, sometimes seeming to back off a bit in order to take a better run at it, but never, never ceasing. It is at first lovely, uplifting one's spirits, and eventually grows aggravating because it continues to pester and won't go away.

Still, just giving oneself up to the wind is a kind of meditation rarely achieved. Only the present matters, sun, sky, land. Nothing else can be thought. I am in the wind but not of it. It is the most alien thing I know, even as I like to be in it. The wind and I have nothing in common, except as blower and blown, toucher and touched. No recourse, no reply is possible. Is this how the Hebrew God first came to be revealed? I wonder what great wind blows over the desert places.

Suddenly that old Cistercian pull is there, and I know what it is about Conques that I love so much. In Conques everything stands still. There is no extra desire, no compulsion to do something, be somewhere else, hurry on to the next awesome experience. I understand that emptiness and compassion are what Christ was about, what he knew. Emptiness is not world denying, but is the understanding of the person who does not want to exercise his or her will upon the world. In the same way, compassion arises not out of some need to be a do-gooder, but from disinterest, from people by and in whom emptiness is understood.

I think there is truly something about contemplating stones that brings out this understanding. I suppose it is partially because in our eyes they are eternal, even though we are told that they change a great deal. They stand for the enduring truths we stake our lives on, whether or not these come from an external deity or from an inner conviction. That is the stones' *mana*, the power they give us to maintain those truths and come to know them better. At Conques there are many stones to overwhelm and teach: the abbey inside and out, the tympanum, and the enfolding hills with the wind as their voice. Truly this is a sacred place.

CHAPTER 11

— COLOMBA —

Cybèle. *Goddess.*

Mary, Virgin. *Saint.*

Nightingale, Florence. *b. 1830, Florence, Italy; d. 1920, London, England. Led first group of professional nurses to serve with the army in the Crimea, 1854. Established first training school for nurses in England. Considered the founder of modern nursing. First woman to be awarded the Order of Merit.*

Eve. *First woman. b? Eden; d? outside Eden. Married to Adam, mother of Cain and Abel. Introduced sexuality into the world, for which roundly condemned. Her reputation is presently on the mend.*

I have just returned from Paris, a horrible day starting with my mother losing her passport the night before. This required an urgent visit this morning to the embassy for a replacement. All the taxis passing on the streets were taken. Finally I managed to persuade a taxi driver parked beside the hotel to put away his crossword puzzle and take us. He overcharged madly but got us there in time. This was followed by another frantic race, this time to the airport to put her on the plane for Toronto. My emotions had been so churned up during this whole episode that my own return from Toulouse to Campagnac in Mitsi, through the rush hour and the ever-changing autoroute construction, passed like a jaunt to the market.

Then, finally, perfection! I had left for Paris under clouds, and came home to the best of sunny days, and the end of the terrace just right for the sitting. Our field below has not been cut yet, and the grasses are gleaming and bending like spun gold, a gift from Rumpelstiltskin. Surrounding this carefree bit of wastefulness, Alain's vines, a hundred rows of them at least, are now five years old and have the brushed look of velour. Down to my left our neighbour's cherry trees are deep magenta, laden. Then beyond all of us are hills with their raked rows of vines, the odd bare brown oblong, and fields of every conceivable green, marked off by deeper patches of trees leading towards the forest.

When it's fair in southwestern France, it is sublime. This afternoon, sitting on the terrace, all I can think of is how lovely, how utterly lovely! I want to gather it all up and hold it for good. Lines from Wordsworth I heard long ago come into my head: "The holy time is quiet as a nun/Breathless with adoration." Oh yes. Would spring be just this beautiful in Canada, if I were to stop and stare? Probably, but I don't.

Who could have done this justice on canvas? Not van Gogh: this air is not hot enough for him. Monet would have understood the greens, certainly, but craved water and colour. Cézanne would have loved the contours and the greens. Yes, I think it is a pity he didn't come this far west. We could have shown him some hills.

Sitting here I am having what might pass for another medieval thought, set off by Tony Hiss's intriguing book *The Experience of Place*. What makes landscape endearing to us, he says, are qualities of mystery, prospect and refuge. I look around and find all of these. There are the corners of the garden where the stone wall disappears behind the too ebullient trees and bushes. There is the grove below that hides our neighbours' house and terrace. There is the winding road down the hill that allows only a glimpse of the wine-producing Manoir Emeillée. I know but I do not know completely what is hidden there. The prospect from the terrace that I described above is even grander when you look up the hill towards Vaour, where the road curves out of sight at the horizon line, next stop heaven. The sense of refuge is everywhere, not merely in our visibly contained garden, but even in the countryside beyond, where the neatly divided fields are the result of benign carefulness. The wolves are gone, and the snakes are timid.

Medieval theologians saw nature as a mirror in which to contemplate the image of God. That's why Saint Bernard took his monks far away from civilization to the hills, and to the brink of river chasms. It wasn't the human ordering of the world that they were to study, but God's. So here are these three notions of mystery, prospect and refuge, which when I read them struck me as just the right way to describe the landscapes I love. Do they express or point to the divine? I think they do both. My little landscape is too tame to bear all the meanings I think of as ultimate reality: the awesomeness of that mystery is missing here. To remember what creation is all about, though, these notions contemplated in this landscape are not a bad way to proceed. So I will.

I love this thought of M.M. Davy's: "the symbol becomes a verb, transforming the shadowed earth into light, into a land transfigured." She's talking about Romanesque sculpture, but she could be describing my landscape as well.

I found this description of the prospect from his country house by someone who lived in the Auvergne:

It is delightful to sit here and listen to the shrill cicada at noon, the croak of frogs at dusk, the clangour of swans and geese in the early part of the night or the crow of cocks in the dead of it, the ominous voice of rooks saluting the dawn in chorus, or, in the half-light, nightingales fluting in the bushes and swallows twittering under the eaves.

The man who wrote this died in 489. This is hardly a peasant's view of the countryside. Certainly during the Middle Ages most people spent all their waking hours looking at the ground. Peasants, who made up 80 percent of the population almost up to our time, were bent over for hoeing, threshing, planting and harvesting. Women, when not working in the fields, were bent low over cooking fires and cradles and their sewing. Here, today you see many people, usually women, walking with a stick and a permanently stooped back. I watch people working on the vines and in the fields in the valley and even with mechanical help they still have to watch the ground carefully and constantly. Nothing much has changed for the women at home, either, except that gas has mainly replaced wood for the stove. Earth meant toil, misery, fatigue.

In contrast, to look up to the sky, where heaven was, must have been to imagine a life without pains, rheumatism and gloom. I suppose my life is not so very different most of the time. Many afternoons, for instance, when I could be outdoors on an ideal summer day, I am inside cramped over a computer screen. Of course it is not the same: I can go out if I choose, lift my head, take my time absorbing the beauty around me. Peasants worked incessantly, I can work and dream. For me as for them, there is a tremendous delight in shifting from such a narrow, intense, and often unlovely focus to the wideness of the whole arch of the sky. When I think of the restrictions on those peasants' vision, I realize how privileged I am, just to have time to look.

It has been very wet for June. Normally our little field would have been cut by now, but Pilar, with our best interests at heart, has postponed it. She says, if Jean-Pierre had cut it before, it would have grown so much that he would have had to cut it again. No point in paying twice. Cutting this fallow field must seem like a waste anyway. We offered it once to the mayor for his use, but he wasn't interested.

The weather was very wet in the first half of the twelfth century, says John James. Mouldy rye became diseased with something called ergot, and people who ate ergot-infected bread might be afflicted with "holy fire." Those least affected had psychedelic visions, while others saw Jesus or the Virgin, and claimed miracles. Raoul Glaber, a twelfth-century monk and historian, says that people who had visions did not live very long afterwards. However tempting to use the mouldy rye as an explanation, I will not be so reductionist. I feel the same way, hearing this, as I did when I learned that Martin Luther was constipated, and therefore.... The mouldy rye explanation is just another example of a groundling's view of the sacred impossible.

Weather must have been a much more serious problem than it is for us. I hate the extremes, whether heat or cold or sleet or heavy fog, and try to go out as little as possible then. Medieval people had no choice, and were probably soaked to the skin regularly. I try to imagine life without slickers, umbrellas, rubber boots, covered vehicles. Life without fans, ice, bug sprays. Life without parkas, fleecy boots, smoke-free heat, and guns to frighten away the wolves.

Then, to make it worse, what would it be like if you entered a monastery or a hermitage, where whatever possible comforts there were had been removed? Daily civilian life was hardship enough, but holiness insisted on more. So delete the meat, the soft wool, the warm hearth, except for an hour or so during recreation, and put in its place stringent fasting, harsh clothing (the hair shirt is no joke), bare feet and chilblains. We live in cocoons compared to them. No wonder we are unable to look at the world as they do, because we do not feel it the same way.

Our familiar wind in this region is the Autan, which comes in from Africa. It is not as well known as the fabled Mistral of Provence, but its effects are just as powerful. The local wise people say the Autan blows either for three days or three weeks. I have been here for part of the three-week run, and found its behaviour certainly odd. Warm and sometimes gentle, it seems friendly, tame enough. Then it changes its temperament and gathers strength enough to force lighter trees to touch the ground. When I am lying in bed at night hearing it whooshing down the chimneys, it does not take much for my suggestive imagination to believe I am the next protagonist in a Gothic novel. The really daunting aspect of the Autan is that it never stops, day or night. No wonder they say it can drive you crazy. I'm relieved to be snug in my twentieth-century hermitage when it blows

Earlier this week the weather played its game of sympathetic magic. The morning and the early afternoon were everything I'd been hoping for these last two damp and dreary weeks. The sky was crystal clear, the breeze mild (the *vent d'Autan* was going incognito), and the sun's warmth was cosseting, not blistering. A good day to hang out the washing and read a little in a French history book. Valérie arrived just as I began, and while we were chatting and making coffee everything changed. Within minutes, the sun had gone, the wind was whipping the laundry topsy-turvy, and ominous noises were coming from a serious black sky. Suddenly there was hail, small stuff the size of chickpeas, but pelting down in potfulls, enough to do damage to the vines. The hail turned into a downpour, Valérie went home to check the windows, and everything stopped. When I next looked outside, the sun was glowing through the clouds while it rained, and eventually the rain was over and we were back to the perfect summer afternoon. The entire theatrical performance, including stage directions such as, "rush around and try to close all the windows, save the laundry, dry off hair and clothes," took an hour. It struck me that the weather had caught my personality remarkably well, with my thundering, railing (rhymes with hailing), wishful, self-pitying moods engaged in for a few moments, and finally resolved in relieved contentment.

One day as I was hanging out a washing on the line above the stone wall, I disturbed a small snake. He was more upset than I was, and took off quickly through the ivy. The sun had just fallen on his part of the wall, and he was tanning on the leaves when I came along. Later on, trying to concentrate on a book outside I saw five or six tiny lizards doing the same, hanging out on the wall, and darting into the ivy from time to time. Some of them are indistinguishable from the gravel on the terrace, and others are wearing grass green. Can you call this frolicking, I wonder, or is it just their ordinary way of doing their business? I guess so. They never stay around long enough for one to learn what else they're capable of when the sun's not out.

In fine weather, if you stay quietly outside long enough you can discover the real, hidden inhabitants of this place. Tonight at dusk, the time when it is easy to slip into a state of reverie, or mind-evacuation, I am alone on the terrace. The air is so still that I think I can hear the birds in the valley below. Then I realize I am not alone. In the little field next to ours that had just been freshly cut, something flounces into view, turns and waves its signal white flag. With binoculars I can see very well now two large pointed ears flexed above a light brown head with deep button eyes. I watch the rabbit eating.

This is a mysterious process. She takes the end of a long piece of grass and crunches it down like a child eating a piece of pasta. She grazes patiently in one spot for a while, and then bounces suddenly across to another juicy patch far away. Maybe she has fleas. Partway through her meal a bigger rabbit pops up from nowhere. The first bit of business is to rush over to check out what the first diner has discovered, then to tear off to find one's own juicier patch. So begins a lovely tag match, the ritual for this *déjeuner sur l'herbe*. I hope they like this field. They are good company.

Suddenly a large bird flies over my head and theirs, disappearing into the orchard beside them. The rabbits vanish. For several evenings we have heard an owl in our trees. This all adds up to menace from the skies and emergency camouflage and slim pickings for the gentle ground people.

Reading philosophical theory can tell you plenty, but sometimes it takes a pause like this to make you really understand. Here I am in my garden chair discovering belatedly that the human perspective is not the only, or even the major one in this land. I came to sit solitary, thinking it was as quiet as a hermit's cell. Instead I find it as busy as any Saturday marketplace. Rush hour comes at dawn and dusk for the rabbits, the owls and hawks. At other times the aisles between the grass blades are filled with ant traffic, the generous spread of delicate whiteness that is the jasmine vine is poked and prodded by touring bees, and butterflies make their timid inspection of the flowers. All the while the airwaves are loud with beetles, birds and the odd froggy croak. I am Gulliver, a heavy-footed visitor to this highly organized land; they are the true citizens, their ancestry and tenancy much older than mine.

We wonder what the rabbit-sized holes in our garden are, trough-like cavities that you could turn your ankle in. I fill in a few of them just in case. This week we meet the resident, a tiny hedgehog who is sitting by the gate at the front of the house. I bend down and look him in the eye and he looks at me, but does not move. We cross the road and when we look back he is scuttling along the front of the house to our unkempt field, no doubt moving to a new location where he can have peace and quiet undisturbed by such mean-spirited neighbours.

The longer I stay here the more microscopic my vision becomes. That is one of the drawbacks of the active life, that you only have time for the big picture. Here everything matters, great and small. I almost feel as though I should apologize for saying this, it sound so corny and dull, but who can say that the vision of six bees snuffling up nectar in a tiny patch of brilliant fuchsia trefle is any less important or beautiful than a great sweep of land or a roaring ocean? It is all in the point of view.

So here it is, a perfectly silly summer day. The sunny blue sky reminds me of Miró's *El Oro de Azur*, a print of which hangs in one of the bedrooms. The heads of the grasses in our un-mown field are nodding; a magpie has just flown over the vineyard, surveying his *domaine*. Far beneath him a host of butterflies is pirouetting over the tops of the grasses, in assorted holiday colours, pure white, black and white and several variations on café-au-lait and orange. It is so long since I have seen such a thing I had forgotten how delicate and whimsical they could be. Miró's abstract rendering of sun, sky, stars and birds has the same euphoric effect.

Standing on the terrace I become aware that two of the coffee-coloured butterflies are performing a deliberate dance right beside me. Whirling together like two tiny independent cyclones (turning and turning in the widening gyre? that is the idea, but nothing so traumatic) they make their way in tandem away from me and back again, their motion almost frantic, their bodies trembling, as it turns out, with anticipation. Then their circles begin to touch, as one seems to attack the other relentlessly.

Now I realize that my youthful education missed something: I had the birds and the bees (I think), but never the butterflies. It seems to me on this frabjus day that I am directly in the path of a steamy courtship, the lovers simply sidestepping me and carrying on rejoicing. It is over shortly, the pair suddenly exhausted and sinking down, one on the gravel, the other on a chair. They seem half dead, but after a few minutes their wings begin to flutter faintly, and eventually they fly off, separately in different directions. Medieval people compared butterflies to angels. We know better.

Our garden and the fields beyond are filled with birdsong, day and night. While the music in Toulouse appeals to the dominant Cluniac side of me, in Campagnac the Cistercian side is divinely satisfied. For the true professionals are practically on our home ground. For several years now Bob has been insisting that there are nightingales in our valley, that they only start singing about midnight, which is why I never hear them when I go out around 11:00 p.m. John and Margaret were just as keen as we were to hear these legendary birds, but when a late dinner on the terrace brought us almost to midnight and still no nightingales sang, Bob decided that we should try another spot. He'd heard that they really belted it out in another valley close by.

We walked up the road to the small cemetery that sits on the crest of the hill overlooking both valleys. There, sitting on the steps of the mausoleum, we heard them. It is a marvellous song, if you can call it that: there is no line, no refrain. No two phrases seem ever to be repeated, an improvisation of the highest order. The notes are high, flute-like but not breathy, quick and true. I suppose they sang for Olivier Messiaen who loved birdsong: only he could compose to include them so divinely.

The experience is so rare I cannot fit it into my emotional concordance. The sound is too remote from the human, too unlike the contrived instrumental sounds, even though the flute is the closest there is. The effect of being a listener is strange. Here is an entire community living alongside us, with nothing in common between us. What we call rare and exquisite music, they would call, if they could, communication. Two parallel worlds. What do we need from them?

Purity of intention. And they from us? Nothing. Nightingales are the troubadours of paradise. A thicket of nightingales is like having heaven in your ears. We must have stayed there for half an hour. Then we went home to sleep.

The story of San Virila says that the monk became so enchanted with the nightingales' song that he lost track of time, fell into a trance and came to three hundred years later. Not surprising.

Gardens were scarce in the early Middle Ages. All the space within the fortified towns was needed for housing. The first open spaces were markets, and it was not until towns were expanded beyond the walls, and the walls came down later still, that there was room for plants and paths. So, in a very important way, gardens meant undisturbed peace, not just as we think of it, a place for quiet contemplation or sunbathing, but as the result of the end of war, brigandage and tumult. They meant good health, enough to eat, a quiet mind, longer life.

For me the garden seems to be the best place to let my mind wander where it pleases. I suppose this is my sort of holy waste. Gardens are so mythic to every religion, yet what happens in them hardly seems to be the stuff of myth. My garden is full today of blighted roses, curled leaves on the cherries, and massed armies of tiny, orderly bugs on the elderberries. The same old weeds are there, perhaps fewer of one kind, more of another. The grass is patchy as usual, this year supplemented by the finest moss and what our botanist friend Bob calls, unappetizingly, slime. The bay tree. Now there's a story! When we first came here we were pleased to see this fine, tall shrub at the corner of the garden wall. The next year everything froze, and we mournfully considered removing the stump of the bay. Ten years later it has reached the third storey of the house, thick, lushly gleaming, and a sure illustration of the warning that the wicked flourish as the green bay tree. Why does the bay flourish but not our roses? And when will we win the race against the birds who lust after our green figs? Every season we manage to salvage about a dishful.

The trunks of the oldest trees, the lilacs, the tamarisk and an apple, are strangely formed. They come up straight for about a metre, then curve out horizontally for a metre or so more, and then grow straight again. They have the same bent backs as the old farmers who tend them.

This year the lilies are out when we arrive, two long lines of white trumpets trisecting the garden. The scent pours in every window deliciously. Of course nothing is perfect: the snails have munched their way up the stems, taking out all the leaves. I will have to find something of equal beauty to plant in front of them, to hide their poor skeletons.

In medieval symbology the decorative version of the lily, the fleur-de-lys, has many meanings besides the patriotic ones. The most common and best interpretation makes it the bridge between heaven and earth. It is incarnational, representing any manifestation of the divine in the human world. You see it often present in illustrations of the Incarnation, but it does not pertain to Mary alone. Knowing these connections made me give the garden another think. Beside the lily there is the fig tree, the bay tree, the apple, the roses and of course the vines. Was the previous owner who planted all these a medievalist or a biblical gardener? I am going to try adding olives and perhaps a palm. There's one growing in my neighbour's garden. To the medieval gardener the palm was the symbol of Minerva, I have just discovered. More green bridges. We already have Athene's owl in our cherry tree.

As everyone who lives in a warmer clime than frosty old Ontario knows, the green growth is astonishing. Apart from that aggressive bay tree, which has now covered the sundial completely and is towering over the yucca, there is bouncing, exuberant movement in the garden, sideways, upwards, and sliding along the ground to pop up many metres away. The weeds fly about seeding themselves in every vacant spot, and crowd in among the long-established flowers as if they had a right there. This year the shrubs and trees have spread their arms every which way, despite, or because of, having been cut back tidily last year. A barberry, its brilliant orange berries hiding sharp thorns all along its branches, puts out limbs at odd angles every year, trim it as I may. I have decided it really wants to be a tree, so I am going to let it fulfill its true destiny, and transplant it into a tree-shaped space. No shrub in Ontario could ever behave like that. They are too timid and troubled with chilblains.

We have moss, butterflies galore and heart-stopping colours in our garden. We have frogs and nightingales. It cannot be paradise, because there are countless tiny green creatures destroying the leaves on the plum tree. "Colomba" is not yet the target of the ecological disaster that is occurring in other parts of the world, however. Yosemite has lost its frogs, St. Catharines has few butterflies, and moss has been drummed out by pollution. Are we in a time warp here, as I have often thought, about a century behind everyone else? Will all the plagues, viruses and noxious gases and pesticides eventually kill this beauteous place? If it is probable, I don't suppose there is a thing we can do about it. I feel as if I am in a J.G. Ballard anti-utopian novel, poised dumbly waiting for the inescapable to happen.

Yesterday Florence Nightingale came to "Colomba." Not the real person but the heroine of *Florence: The Lady with the Lamp*. This Florence is a strong woman driven both by her own need to make something of her life and by her vision of the good she must do. She is sharp, easily roused to anger and goads people relentlessly to do what she believes is needed. At the same time she is tossed about emotionally by her love for her family, their scandalized view of her choice of career, and her dedication to the care of wounded soldiers. At the end of the opera, back from the Crimea, a more mature Florence questions the selflessness of her own goals but is assured by her friend that her sometimes misguided efforts were certainly worth it.

I have repeatedly said that the part of me that is Florence does not travel to Campagnac. I believe that the reason for this is the lack of conflicting pressures and the build-up of stress that produces this noisy, rousing, emphatic and bloody-minded character in Canada. Without them I am a tamer pussycat, untroubled by opposing needs and forces, able to give myself to the present in a contemplative way, without anxieties about tomorrow.

Then yesterday I got angry, really and truly white-hot. The causes seem petty, silly even today; yesterday they turned me into a pillar of rage. I couldn't move, waiting to let the feeling tell me what to do. Where could I go, what could I do to express this anger? I went into the garden. The thinking part of me said that now would be a good time to work out my anger in some physical way, to cut off all the dead irises and lilacs, for instance. The emotional part of me wanted to cut off all the lily buds, the roses, everything beautiful and new. Reason began to take over: I decided to start with the dead stuff, and if the feeling still persisted I would go on to the lilies. I cut and chopped for an hour, feeling more and more infuriated. Finally I cut off needlessly a couple of rose branches that were in my way. Seeing these beauties on the ground, I realized this was undeserved destruction, and stopped. It seemed to finish the episode.

I cannot imagine why I wanted to ruin the most beautiful plants in my garden. I came so close. I can still feel the vibrations of that anger in my arms, my stomach and my head. The meaning must be very important, certainly beyond its trivial causes. I will let this go for the moment, but perhaps it is only in Campagnac, where such blithe contemplation can happen, that other feelings are brought up from one's real centre, matters that are usually covered over with thoughts, pale and thick. I recall that Florence brought back from the Crimea a small owl she kept in her pocket called Athene. Perhaps it was her contemplative touchbird.

In pre-medieval thought the *hortus conclusus*, the enclosed garden, represents the Virgin Mary; by the twelfth century it has also come to mean the soul. That is the lovely thing about symbols, how one trails into another. You could never say, for instance, that the Virgin Mary and the soul were equivalent, or homologous. You can say that there are traces of the same fragrance about them. What could it be? Purity, single-mindedness and, I suppose, devotion.

With this symbol Mary replaces Eve as the inhabitant of the garden. Exit Mother of All Living, enter Mother of God. The garden remains pristine. That is not my garden, but perhaps it is the garden within my garden, the innate, wonderful created thing that we call the soul. If so then Eve's soul, which is much closer to mine after all than Mary's is, is still there in the garden, beside the jasmine, playing with the lizards on my wall. A statue of Cybèle here beside the wall would be a nice finishing touch.

Renaissance garden lovers saw them as polyvalent symbols, as nostalgic places, reminders of the lost Eden, but also as places for reverie, trysts and thoughts of death. Probably they were the first people to look at a garden as a thing of beauty. Apparently when Petrarch, the poet and great lover, climbed Mont Ventoux near Orange to look at the view sometime in the fourteenth century, it was considered a very peculiar thing to do. The idea of taking pleasure in a landscape was just arriving in the mind's eye.

Structurally speaking, the garden and the wilderness are symbolic opposites. You have innocence versus experience, order against chaos, enclosure versus openness, the known versus the unknown. The interesting thing about these oppositions is that the direction of activity is not always one way. Although there is no possibility of going back to innocence, or of moving from the unknown to the previously known – the garden of Eden is sealed off – you can move freely from order to chaos, enclosure to openness and vice versa. Something, but not all, of the mythical garden of the first days of existence is recapturable; the wilderness can be entered anytime. They interact with each other.

Perhaps that is why attempts at the perfect garden are foiled, usually by being sterile, predictable, tight. When one looks at them, there is nowhere for the mind to follow the senses into some reverie or revelation. One could say that a Versailles must lead to a revolution, which is a kind of wilderness. Too simple? Of course! This is only a model. Reality is an ever-shifting compound of the two symbols.

For me the garden is a useful analogy for our particular way of living. There is hardship in the garden, and cruelty; there is joy and benediction; there is struggle, repetitious, never-ending; there is rest and contemplation; sun and shade, drought and downpour. All the extremes of living meet here, or follow one another in quick steps. The garden cannot truly be tamed; it will always rise to greet us in its own willed ways. We should be glad that it doesn't behave slavishly to us. Not many things provide such a model for living. Here, creation does what comes naturally and, I believe, supernaturally. I guess I really cannot find much difference between my garden and the wilderness; they abide together.

I found a quotation from Gregory of Nyssa: "O man, when you consider the universe, you understand your own nature."

Reliquaries St. Trophine Arles

CHAPTER 12

— CONCLUSION —

I f I could isolate one striking cause of the change in my religious attitude in the last decade or more, I would choose my immersion in this happy secularity that embraces the sacredness of ordinary living. Most of the French are not religious today. Their medieval ancestors, however, made no distinction between sacred and secular acts. Everyday life was full of rituals, and religion was the overarching story that interpreted them, gave them meaning. In some way that I cannot quite sum up yet, my life in Campagnac follows that eleventh-century pattern.

There is a qualitative difference between the performance of even the most ordinary tasks here and the same jobs in Canada. What is unconsciously matter-of-fact in St. Catharines is the subject of alert concentration here, the awareness of the actual business of doing the work at hand. Heidegger says that you only know the being of some-thing such as a hammer when it is broken. I think you can begin to know it when, for instance, the handle of a spade weighs so much more than its Canadian counterpart, or when you chop off the head and feet of the chicken you bought at the market. These differences let you in on the meaning of things. They become rituals: closing the shutters at night, going to meet the bread truck, shaking hands with the restaurant owner you know.

I have watched women tirelessly picking over the potatoes at a market stall, rejecting most of those I'd have blithely taken. I have been invited into the chilly front room of a farmhouse to take an apéritif at the grand table covered with a lace cloth, clearly a special arrangement for the unusual guest. Once I was told, after being conducted painstakingly through the farmyard, into the greenhouse and over the fields to see the rabbits in another barn, that I had made what is called *la grande visite*. And I have seen and heard, as has everyone who has ever travelled in France, the warm conviviality of a group of friends gathered along the bar for a *pastis* after work. The cadences of their voices and the sounds of their laughter seem never to vary from one brasserie to another.

The art critic John Berger, writing about Zurburán's *The Holy House of Nazareth*, says that the sense of sacredness in the picture comes, not from the image of angels nor from symbolism, but from the way he paints domestic objects and tasks as bearers of meaning. "Everything he paints looks as if it is eternal.... Everything with which we surround our- selves feels as if it's disposable." When you're doing everyday things repeatedly but in a strange place, you can see them for what they are, rituals that preserve a kind of fragile social barrier against the threats of a civilization becoming more and more uncivilized. That's the com- ment of a moralizing amateur sociologist: the other side of the coin is, the care of domestic things that becomes ritualized is in some way good in itself, done for no practical reason. Holy waste.

Whenever my grandmother used to catch me rushing through a boring kitchen job, she'd say, to my annoyance, the old cliché: "If a thing's worth doing, it's worth doing well." In Campagnac I can at last see why she was right.

France is not for every day. It is my country for special feelings, the time set aside from what I have to do to attend to what I want to do, what I think really matters. Living here is for taking time to reflect on what has taken place: personally, socially, politically, religiously, but most of all personally. Being in Campagnac is the time and place for let- ting everything I've done catch up with what it means. It's the place and time for putting my actions into a context, either an old inherited one, or a new one brought about by contemplation in the present. According to one medievalist's definition, this is part of what it means to go on pilgrimage. The other part I think has to do with one's emotions.

Despite what I like to believe, it is my right-brain thinking that usually determines the left. Even though I'm so damn rational most of the time, there's another daimon driving me, out of some centre of my being. When that daimon is not permitted to shout, scream or even whisper, I get tight, controlled, cool. Reading about the character of twelfth-century people I discover that they were governed by their emotions. They were easily aroused, subject to what we would call mood swings, prone to violence, but also to religious fervour. Pope Urban II resorted to tears when preaching the First Crusade; no doubt his audience burst into floods too, and signed up.

Pilgrimage was a time when the immediacy of one's experience and its validity shone out. When I read that pilgrims had no problems with venerating the relics of the same saint in two separate neighbouring locations, I thought it was a sure test of cognitive dissonance. If it came to the question, I suppose a devotee would argue that a show of many parts from the same saint demonstrated God's largesse and the saint's powerfulness. Deity beats logic hands down. People today couldn't handle it. We, meaning even the most apperceptive people I know, modify our sensuous experiences by filtering them through our intellects. Often I move so quickly from sensation to analysis I hardly have a truly direct experience of what's around me at all.

Here, though, I amble around house, garden and village, feeling sunny inside. It is the same intense experience I used to have years ago when I became absorbed in contemplation, only this time there is no chosen object to think about. I am in the object. In fact, the subject-object split almost disappears.

While "Colomba" has up until recently seemed to be a holiday house, away from all the everydayness of Canada, in the last year or so some overlapping has been taking place. The lovely idyll that is Campagnac and all that surrounds it has been infiltrated by thoughts of Canada. Of course we always speak of home, the children, our work, our projects, our friends, but almost in the same dreamlike way that we think of Campagnac, the fantasy-in-operation, when we are not there. We phone back and forth to the kids, to John to inquire about the dog and the house, with a shockingly expensive regularity. So it is not as though we are bound into a little cocoon, only to emerge on the transatlantic return flight. I am more and more connected to my Canadian life. I work by fax and phone on projects, talk to friends, worry about things I used to ignore till my return. In other words the feeling of what is home is becoming a transatlantic affair.

I haven't really thought a great deal about home until recent years. Home was always a taken-for-granted thing. It hardly rose to the status of an idea because it wasn't problematic. Home has always been the place where we are, this little family which began as two, became five, and shrank to two again. (It always amazes and pleases me when the kids talk about "coming home" still, when they all have perfectly good homes of their own.) Home is about the people who dwell within it first and foremost, but it is also about the shape and contents and location of the particular house we are in at the time. I have house fantasies: there are types of houses that I would dearly love to live in, because they offer different sorts of living. My favourite is modelled on Frank Lloyd Wright's masterpiece, Fallingwater, the interior of which is completely open, with a fireplace, books, plants, a broad kitchen and a pool. Not much more. The outside is pure Wright and descends firmly down the hillside, following a woodland stream. The fantasy, of course, is relaxation, meditation and food for the body as well as the mind. The reality is, and I certainly know it, that the house does not shape the life but vice versa.

Just as I am thinking that it is the pilgrimage that shapes one's home, I come across Eliade's definition of home in earlier preliterate societies as the intersection of vertical and horizontal poles, the gods and the dead meeting the activity of one's life. Outside that meeting place, he says, is the unreal, chaos; for me that would be the wilderness, the not-yet place out of which one may draw meaning. Home, although not perhaps in a physical sense for people today, is still the centre where everything comes together. St. Bernard disparages the idea of going on a pilgrimage, saying that the real centre of pilgrimage is one's own heart. I think Berger would agree. Even if that is true, I think the pilgrimage is a way of making that discovery. Like T.S. Eliot, I think that "the end of all our exploring/Will be to arrive where we started/And know the place for the first time."

I saw in Paris recently a strangely compelling exhibition of Italian artist Luciano Fabro's constructions called *Habitat*. As I passed through, under or alongside each of them, I found that delicate, infinitesimal changes were taking place in me. I had the desire to make something new, something that mattered, to pass through present barriers, ones I thought were social. Later, reading the catalogue, I learn that Fabro says, "The artist is not changing the world at the end of history, but at the beginning, in the person." Home is the heart.

Then I saw the sacred link I have made between the two houses we call home, French and Canadian. There are two contrasting sets of religiosity that I might assign to myself: there is the Cluniac/Cistercian, treasure-the-world vs. withdraw-from-it division; and there is the meditative/contemplative approach to spirituality. Meditation enables us to focus intensely on an object, an idea, or even on emptiness itself, in order to reach through the symbol to the reality beyond. Contemplation takes the world as its symbol, spreading its gaze far and wide. Both paths have their value; both can lead one astray. These two paths may overlap but do not coincide.

Today I cannot meditate using a single focus because the notion of hierarchy is wrong for me. I can try to empty my thoughts and focus on nothing, but that is difficult for me practically speaking, though not theologically. Contemplation suits me now, and seems to carry me forward. What began with this pilgrimage as a rather narrow, intellectual approach – looking at Romanesque buildings – opened up of itself to include the saints, their antecedent colleagues, the cities they dwelt in, the fields and forests they may have walked through. Then it came back to Campagnac. Now I can take it home to Canada, inside me, where I am so taken up with my Cluniac ways, for good or ill, that I have no time for the Cistercian longings within me. I am confident, though, that the lessons I learn in one home carry over to the other, because I am the carrier. As long as I do not forget.

I am beginning to make sense of all that I have seen and thought. First of all, I realize that, just as it was for many in the twelfth century, orthodoxy is not for me. I do not really believe in One God (Male), One Church (Male driven) and One Faith. Neither would I believe in One God (Female) etc. I do, though, believe in God, holy, beyond imaging, towards whom we direct our attention, our thought, our lives. I can both address this god as You, and at the same time realize that I am now moving at another level, into the realm of images. This god is both unqualified and yet manifested through all sorts of images and symbols.

This isn't new, even to Christianity. It is essential Paul Tillich, though my particular interpretation owes a lot to the philosophical school of Hinduism called Advaita Vedanta. (In both cases, this is my reading of these systems; I make no claim to be an expert, nor to say that this is the only reading.) Ever since I studied Tillich in the 1970s, I've thought myself to be a Tillichian. The problem was, I didn't know how to take this basic belief in ultimate reality as the Ground of Being and apply it to what I was already immersed in: the church, with its forms of prayer and worship. I still don't, but the problem has shifted a bit, and I can now come at it from another place.

I've always hated the grovelling aspect of Christianity, never felt myself to be a miserable sinner – sinner yes, miserable no. I really believe that we can do better, not that we are condemned to rot in our wickedness, only to be yanked out of the pit by a compassionate, just God. I think that nature is basically good, that there was never a fortunate fall, that evil is not our first inclination but the consequence of lots of other things. This is the aspect of Christian theology that I have never truly subscribed to, even when I was behaving at my grovelling worst.

Jesus I knew was certainly the answer, both to our anxiety about goodness and our need to understand where we were headed and why. I loved him as a lover might, speaking to him conversationally and believing that the faithful discoveries I made came from him. My faith was wonderfully lively and joyful. No more grovelling.

Then other problems arose, in particular the need to uncover the feminist position in the church, and in theology. First I had to find out what the situation was, and then see what if anything was being done about it. As I went along, my connection with the worshipping life of the church dwindled. Everywhere I turned I was struck by the lack of attention to feminist concerns, or the namby-pamby attempts to cater to them. At the same time, the sense of male dominance persisted, in every vocal activity, including the speech of people who should have been more aware, I thought.

I told Jesus I was not abandoning him, but I had to take a break. I couldn't just carry on as though nothing else was on my mind. I said, "I'll be back."

I read feminist theology, feminist work about goddesses in antiquity, in contemporary spirituality, in one's psyche. Most of it I thought was silly, argumentative, ignorant. Some of the theology and archaeology excited me. Nothing struck me as completely satisfying.

Then I began this pilgrimage through the Romanesque world. Although I had no conscious intention of dealing with my own religious situation, there was a niggling little hope, a tiny crack in my aesthetic shell that said, maybe. Maybe the twelfth century has something to pass on today. After all, it was a period of renaissance; why not a small rebirth for me?

Reading about this period gave me a good clue. Matters were just as mixed up religiously then as now. Women were in deep trouble just for being women, but there were a few lights. Besides, there were men who did not agree with the orthodox line about the wickedness of all women. They were the voices that had been silenced over the years. Of course the whole history was politically charged, as it still is today.

As I went to these marvellous Romanesque sites I began to do what every person, from the humblest to the most theologically acute, does: look at the buildings, listen to the histories, read the arguments, and select what I could use for my situation today. We now know that long ago the lives of the saints were modelled on standard formulae derived from the funeral orations of the Greeks and Romans. To get at the factuality of these lives would be impossible; for the life of faith it is unnecessary. The Mary Magdalene who was worshipped is the "true" one, even if she never existed. She is the model, perhaps the archetype, used by the church for devotional purposes for hundreds of years. She is probably derived from other, older models. Or perhaps she was a new invention of the church to coincide with a new idea of woman and of piety.

It is certainly time to question the usefulness and veracity of these old models. What I am beginning to do is to draw from the old narratives some new possibilities, to reinterpret the images of these strong, influential women and men for our own time. I have no doubt that this has been done by hundreds of others over the centuries and is being done right now by many, many more.

Then I found other women who have been worshipped or at least revered in the West since mythologies have been known. Lost, denied and condemned, they are now being discovered, admired and in some cases exalted. Their attributes are necessary to us; the meaning of these women's lives must be part of the contemporary religious mixture.

The church today is talking about being more inclusive. Which being interpreted somewhat callously yet truthfully is: we are down to the last cluster of middle- and old-age whiteys, mostly middle-class Anglo-Saxons and Celts, and we need to bring in others in order to stay alive. So somehow we must attract the young, blacks, divorced, families, immigrants, in fact all the people with whom Jesus wanted to share the good news, or would have if such groups had been part of the Palestinian scene. Good. I don't suppose anyone has any idea as to how we are going to do this, without changing anything else. Because I haven't heard much about any other sort of change.

I am working on inclusiveness also, but it's not the same at all. I do think, for instance, that Christianity is both monotheistic and poly-theistic at the same time. Those saints and the ancient gods of the West are symbolic of the divine being, who is one. Jesus as part of a Trinity is a construction I neither need nor can figure out at present. He is, however, the great revelation of the divine to the Jews, who said no thanks, and to those who accept him.

Jesus is the great symbol, the great hope, the sun, the phoenix. His resurrection is in all of us who take hold of life in the way in which he points us. The words, "I am the way, the truth and the life" are ascribed to him with great accuracy. He is the superb lover of God, of people of every stripe. He believes in the ability of humanity to overcome death, the fear of it, the way it drives our lives. He shows us how.

One by one, the saints along with the rest of us pick up part of his message, part of his role and behaviour, and carry along the task of changing the world.

I seem to be back where I started from about thirty years ago. Not quite: I have widened my focus, and become a whole lot happier. What's the next step, I wonder? This journey's neverending, and never dull.

I have completed another stage of this pilgrimage, which began years and years ago, in Toronto, Windsor, Fonthill, St. Catharines, Guelph, Elora. In going through the wilderness there have been many wells: people, churches, retreats, music. There has been prayer and meditation, reading and the academic study of religion. When the trips to France began, there were Vézelay, Autun, Bourges, Chartres, right at the start. There was the visit to L'Arche.

Then there were the children, all born just before we started travelling. Beautiful people all through their lives (the memory discards all the days of panic, the temper tantrums – theirs and mine – the anxiety, and the too-much-to-look-after feelings), they are refreshing, nourishing wells.

Always there is Bob, partner in everything, with the exception of this weird, zigzag thinking that permeates this writing, for which he's not responsible. After more than forty years, we still love almost all the same things, people, music, France, and each other.

Coming here was a new beginning, an unreclaimed house, a community about which we knew nothing, no friends, no helpers, and very weak French. I did all the things I normally loathe, like painting, digging, staining, and loved it. We spent much of our time in Canada planning what we would do, and where our next little trip would be.

We were not new, though. Along with our skills, our good humour and delight in everything, we brought our usual awkwardness, naïveté and ignorance. The one thing we left behind is the stress of life in the middle lane. It can wait.

Going on pilgrimage to these remarkable sites is both a mirror of my life's pattern and a real part of my life, just as living in Campagnac and living in St. Catharines is. What I have time to think about and do here, I merely sputter about in Canada. This is the place where breathing in and breathing out become foremost. It is spiritual therapy. It is using the wilderness for a well. You go there to find the sacred stones and touch them, not really knowing what to hope for. Maybe, as sculptor John Greer said to me, "we're all just stardust anyway." That's not such a bad ending. Or maybe there is another truth blowin' in the wind.

On the journey that was to become his last here on earth, Thomas Merton wrote: "Suddenly there is a point where religion becomes laughable. Then you decide that you are nevertheless religious...." All those weird saints, those bits and pieces of holy bodies, those grotesque carvings, those snakes and butterflies, those lurking god-desses. Those struggling pilgrims dead set on going to the end, only to discover they have already arrived. Alice and the Red Queen running backwards to stay at the beginning. Me – going away in order to come home.

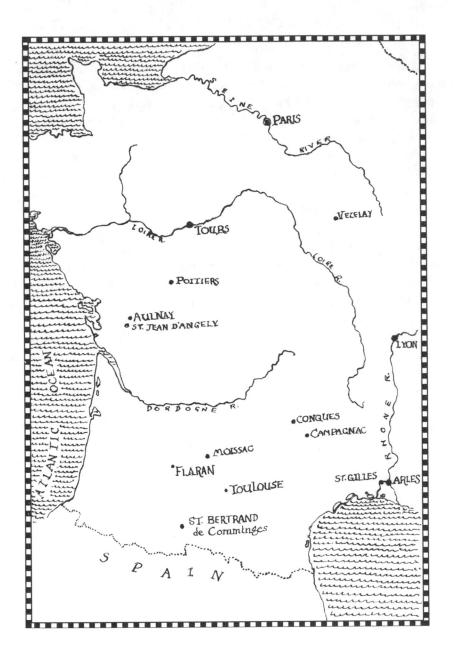

— EPILOGUE —

I can mark my pilgrimage by some particular friends who have travelled it with me: drawing me forward when I was unwilling to take another step; showing me how to take off the blinkers I'd been wearing and look afresh; turning a cold, harsh light on my old ideology and fantasy-making, and showing me the dangerous road ahead. There have been many other strong fellow pilgrims; these few, however, are my "saints," my close companions along the way. Without them I would have turned away from the path. Some of them are now walking in a greater light.

Madeleine Davis Louise Rockman

Ernest Harrison Clare Slater

Harry Mansfield Ralph Spence

John Mays Harold Thomasson

Helen Milton

— WORKS CONSULTED —

Barral i Altet, Xavier. *Compostelle: le grand chemin*. Paris: Gallimard, 1993.

Barret, Pierre & Gurgand, Jean-Noël. *Priez pour nous à Compostelle*. Paris: Hachette, 1978.

Benazech, Yves. "Le 17 août 1944, le combat de 'Marssac,'" in *Revue du Tarn*, No. 134, été, 1989, pp. 297-309.

Berger, John. *And Our Faces, My Heart, Brief as Photos*. New York and Toronto: Random House, Vintage, 1991.

— *Keeping a Rendezvous*. New York: Vintage Books, 1992.

Bernard, Thomas, o.p. & Vesco, Jean-Luc, o.p. *Marie de magdala: évangiles et traditions*. Paris: Éditions Saint-Paul, 1982.

Bloch, Marc. *French Rural History: An Essay on Its Basic Characteristics*, tr. Janet Sondheimer. Berkeley and Los Angeles: University of California Press, 1966.

Braudel, Fernand. *The Identity of France*, tr. Siân Reynolds. London: Fontana Press, 1989.

Brissaud, Yves-Bernard. *Patrimoine de Poitiers: deux millénaires d'art & d'histoire*. Brissaud, 1993.

Brunel-Lobrichon, Geneviève et Duhamel-Amado, Claudie. *Au temps des troubadours: XIIe-XIIIe siècles*. Paris: Hachette, 1997.

Calkins, Robert G. *Monuments of Medieval Art*. New York: E.P Dutton, 1979.

Cunneen, Sally. *In Search of Mary: The Woman and the Symbol*. New York and Toronto: Ballantine Books, 1996.

Davis-Weyer, Caecilia. *Early Medieval Art 300-1150*. Toronto: University of Toronto/Medieval Academy of America, 1986.

Davy, M.M. *Initiation à la symbolique romane*. Paris: Flammarion, 1977.

Delaruelle, Chanoine É. *Saint-Bertrand*. Zodiaque, 1987.

Denis, Jean-Pierre. *Histoires de Choeur: Saint-Bertrand-de-Comminges, les Stalles et l'Orgue*. Toulouse: Le Pérégrinateur, 1995.

Desforges, Dominique. *Arles et la Camargue: le guide.* Tournai: Editions Casterman, 1997.

Dossat, Yves. "Types exceptionnels de pèlerins: l'hérétique, le voyageur déguisé, le professionel," in *Cahiers de Fanjeaux 15: Le pèlerinage,* ed. Édouard Privat. Toulouse: Centre d'Études historique de Fanjeaux, 1980, pp. 207-225.

Duby, Georges. *L'An Mil.* Paris: Éditions Gallimard/Julliard, 1980.

— *Dames du XII° siècle. 1. Héloise, Aliénor, Iseut et quelques autres.* Paris: Editions Gallimard, 1995.

— III. *Ève et les prêtes.* Paris: Éditions Gallimard, 1996.

— *The Knight, the Lady and the Priest: The Making of Modern Marriage in Medieval France,* tr. Barbara Bray. New York and Toronto: Pantheon, Random House, 1983.

— *Le Moyen Âge. Adolescence de la Chrétienté occidentale 980-1140.* Genève: Éditions d'Art Albert Skira S.A., 1995.

— *L'Europe des Cathédrales 1140-1280.* Genève: Éditions d'Art Albert Skira S.A., 1995.

Dupront, Alphonse. *Du Sacre: Croisades et pèlerinages, images et langages.* Paris: Gallimard, 1987.

Durliat, M. *La sculpture romane de la route de Saint-Jacques: de Conques à Compostelle.* Mont-de-Marsan: Comité d'Etudes sur l'Histoire et l'Art de la Gascogne, 1990.

Eliade, Mircea. *Patterns in Comparative Religion.* Cleveland and New York: The World Publishing Company, 1966.

Festinger, Lionel. *When Prophecy Fails.* Minneapolis: University of Minnesota Press, 1956.

Fraternités Monastiques de Jérusalem. *Vézelay.* Paris: Communion de Jérusalem, 1995.

Gardère, Michel. *Ultréïa! le printemps des pierres.* Portet-sur-Garonne: Loubatières, 1993.

Gérard, Pierre. *Pèlerins de Compostelle au Moyen-Âge.* Archives départementales de la Haute-Garonne, n.d.

Guide bleu Midi-Pyrénées. Paris: Hachette, 1989.

Guirand, Félix and Schmidt, Joël. *Mythes & Mythologie.* Paris: Larousse, 1996.

Gurevich, Aron. *Medieval Popular Culture,* tr. János M. Bak and Paul A. Hollingsworth. Cambridge: Cambridge University Press, 1988.

Hiss, Tony. *The Experience of Place*. New York: Alfred A. Knopf, 1990.

Histoire de la France des orgines à nos jours. Sous la direction de Georges Duby. Paris: Larousse, 1995.

Histoire de l'Église Saint Hilaire. Poitiers, 1986.

Huchet, Patrick. *Les chemins de Compostelle en terre de France*. Rennes: Editions Ouest-France, 1997.

Huizinga, J. *The Waning of the Middle Ages*. Garden City, New York: Doubleday & Company, Inc., 1954.

James, John. *The Traveler's Key to Medieval France: A Guide to the Sacred Architecture of Medieval France*. New York: Knopf, 1986.

James, Henry. *A Little Tour in France*. New York: Farrar, Strauss & Giroux, 1983.

Kelly, Amy. *Eleanor of Aquitaine and the Four Kings*. Cambridge, Massachusetts and London, England: Harvard University Press, 1977.

Kingwell, Mark. *Dreams of Millennium: Report from a Culture on the Brink*. Toronto: Viking, 1996.

Kümmel, Werner Georg. *Introduction to the New Testament*, tr. A.J. Martill, Jr. Nashville & New York: Abingdon Press, 1966.

Laborde-Balen, Louis and Rob Day. *Le chemin de St-Jacques du Puy en-Velay à Roncevaux*. Randonnées Pyrénéennes and Fédération Française de la Randonnée Pédestre, n.d.

— *Le chemin d'Arles vers Saint Jacques de Compostelle*. Randonnées Pyrénéennes and Fédération Française de la Randonnée Pédestre, Tarbes: 1990.

Le Goff, Jacques. *La civilisation de l'occident médiéval*. Les Éditions Arthaud, Paris: 1984.

— *Les intellectuals au Moyen Age*. Paris: Éditions du Seuil, 1957.

Leloup, Jean-Yves. *L'Évangile de Marie*. Paris: Albin Michel, 1997.

Le Roy Ladurie, Emmanuel. *Histoire du Languedoc*. Paris: Presses Universitaires de France, 1962.

— *Montaillou: The Promised Land of Error*, tr. Barbara Bray. New York and Toronto: Vintage, Random House, 1979.

Lerner, Gerda. *The Creation of Feminist Consciousness: From the Middle Ages to Eighteen-seventy*. New York: Oxford University Press, 1993.

Lowell, Robert. *Collected Prose*. New York: Farrar, Straus, Giroux, 1987.

Markale, Jean. *Mélusine*. Paris: Éditions Retz, 1983.

Merton, Thomas. *The Asian Journal of Thomas Merton*. New York: New Directions, 1975.

— *Conjectures of a Guilty Bystander*. New York: Doubleday, 1966.

— *The Seven Storey Mountain*. Toronto: The New American Library of Canada Limited, 1963.

Morris, Colin. *The Discovery of the Individual 1050-1200*. Toronto, Buffalo, London: University of Toronto Press, 1995.

Mumford, Lewis. *The City in History*. New York: Harcourt, Brace and World, 1961.

Nicolson, Adam. *The Elf Book of Long Walks in France*. London: George Weidenfeld and Nicolson Ltd, 1985.

Otto, Rudolf. *The Idea of the Holy*, tr. John W. Harvey. New York: Oxford University Press, 1950.

Oursel, Raymond. *Pèlerins du Moyen Age*. Paris: Librairie Arthème Fayard, 1978.

— *Univers roman*. Office du Livre, 1964.

Pacaut, Marcel. *L'Ordre de Cluny*. Paris: Librairie Arthème Fayard, 1986.

Pagels, Elaine. *The Gnostic Gospels*. New York: Vintage, Random House, 1981.

Panofsky, Erwin. *Renaissance and Renascences*. New York, Hagerstown, San Francisco, London: Harper & Row, 1972.

Paul, Jacques. *L'Église et la culture en occident IX-XII siècles*. Tome 2, *L'éveil évangelique et les mentalités religieuses*. Paris: Presses Universitaires de France, 1986.

Pernoud, Georges et Régine. *Le tour de France médiéval*. Paris: Éditions Stock, 1982.

Pernoud, Régine. *La femme au temps des croisades*. Paris: Éditions Stock/Laurence Pernoud,1990.

Petzold, Andreas. *Le monde roman*. Paris: Flammarion, 1995.

Plaskow, Judith and Christ, Carol P., eds.*Weaving the Visions: New Patterns in Feminist Spirituality*. San Francisco: Harper SanFrancisco, 1989.

Pressouyre, Léon. *Le rêve cistercien*. Paris: Gallimard/Caisse nationale des Monuments historiques et des Sites, 1993.

Quéré, France. *La Femme et les Pères de l'Église*. Paris: Desclée de Brouwer, 1997.

Ramball, Paul. *French Blues: A Journey in Modern France*. London: Heinemann-Mandarin, 1989.

Reuss, Henry and Margaret. *The Unknown South of France: A History Buff's Guide*. Boston: The Harvard Common Press, 1991.

Rispa, Raúl; de los Rios, César Alonso; Aguaza, Maria José, eds. *XVème Siècle*. Milano: Sociedad Estatal para la Exposición Universal Sevilla 92, Sevilla and Electa, 1992.

Rouquette, Jean-Maurice and Sintès, Claude. *Arles antique*. Ministère de la culture, de la communication, des grands travaux et du Bicentenaire, 1989.

Saalman, Howard. *Medieval Architecture*. New York: George Braziller, 1965.

Schapiro, Meyer. *The Sculpture of Moissac*. New York: George Braziller, Inc., 1985.

Sévère, Sulpice. *Vie de saint Martin*. Paris: Les Éditions du Cerf, 1996.

Steiner, George. *In Bluebeard's Castle*. London: Faber and Faber, 1971.

Tillich, Paul. *The New Being*. New York: Charles Scribner's Sons, 1955.

Tonnellier, Chanoine. *Aulnay de Saintonge*. Saintes: Delavaud, n.d.

Vieillard, Jeanne. *Le guide du pèlerin de Saint-Jacques de Compostelle*. Paris: Librairie Philosophique J. Vrin, 1984.

de Voragine, Jacques. *La Légende Dorée*, tr. J.-B.M. Roze. Paris: GF-Flammarion, 1967.

Warner, Marina. *Alone of All Her Sex: The Myth and Cult of the Virgin Mary*. New York: Random House, 1983.

Williams, Charles. *Descent into Hell*. William B. Eerdmans, Grand Rapids, MI: n.d.

Williams, Marty and Echols, Anne. *Between Pit and Pedestal: Women in the Middle Ages*. Princeton: Markus Wiener Publishers, 1993.